Brussels
in Sips and Steps

Starting Points of Walks

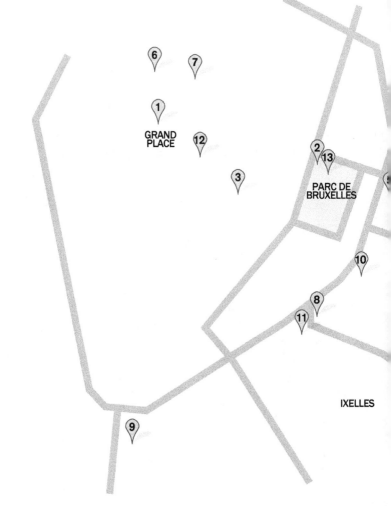

PARC DU CINQUANTENAIRE

(14)

(4)

Brussels
in Sips and Steps

Fourteen Self-Guided Walks to Explore
Brussels' History and Belgium's Beers

W S Comstock

Printed in the United States of America

ISBN 978-1-7326556-0-7

Library of Congress Control Number 2018909903

ITravelInsideOut Publishing House

Design and layout: Laura Haass

To my Bruzzels

Brussels in Steps and Steps
Table of Contents

Foreword

Why a book of walking tours in Brussels?

Like other business people, government officials and journalists, I frequently came to Brussels as its importance grew with its hosting of European Union institutions. At first my visits were limited to the EU quarter, Avenue Louise and the Grand Place. As time went on, I explored, visiting the upper town and then the Art Nouveau districts of Ixelles, Schaerbeek, and Saint-Gilles. I rode the tram in one direction, visiting the early to mid-20th Century suburbs, and then rode in the other direction to see the working-class neighborhoods that formed the backbone of 19th Century Brussels.

I discovered a city with living pictures of its past hidden down alleys and around the next corner. Even with urban plans that seemed like good ideas at the time but swallowed neighborhoods and buildings, Brussels has preserved its past, sometimes by a piece here and another there. My walks aimed at finding them.

Walk the boulevards of Paris and you will find cafes with neatly arranged small tables, each with two chairs. In Brussels, the tables and chairs are scattered about on the sidewalk, moved to where they are needed. Function takes precedence over form; living trumps formality; interaction is expected.

Walk one block and you will find a remnant of the 16th Century when Brussels was a crucial point along trade routes of the time, a prize fought for by the French and the Spanish. Walk another and you will see the Brussels that was the capital of one of the 19th Century's richest countries, a city whose leading citizens fueled the Continent's industrial revolution with coal, steel and rubber and whose liberal constitution nurtured freedom of expression, manifested in art, industrial innovation and architecture. Walk the city and you see a haphazard combination of progress and neglect, but always a city that is alive.

As I explored Brussels, I asked how this or that came to be and why this or that is here. Since Brussels is a city where people socialize and enjoy beer, I was not without the opportunity to make new acquaintances anxious to share their experiences. Through them, I connected the dots to discover the rich mosaic that is Brussels. Always, it was over a beer served in a glass marked with the name of the brewer. As the brewmaster at a Belgian brewery once told me, "Beer is our heritage. We take pride in serving it properly."

Introduction

Using the Guide

- **Starting Points.** Walks begin at Metro stations but you don't have to take the Metro to get to them. At their conclusion, walks point you to a Metro or tram for the return. Most walks start and end at points that are within walking distance of major hotels.

- **Metro and Tram.** Several walks include segments on public transport to save steps. The Brussels Card includes entry to selected museums and unlimited mass transit access for a specified number of days. It can be bought in museums, Brussels tourist offices or online. If you want to skip the museums, buy a 24-hour or "Jump" Ticket at a Metro kiosk or ticket window at some tram stops. The Jump Ticket lets you get on and off trams, buses and Metro as often as you like during a 24-hour period.

- **Walk Length.** An estimated time of completion is provided for each walk. These estimates exclude museums and Debriefing Points. Beers, boulettes, moules, and Flemish stews will extend a walk considerably. Of course, enjoying them is why you are in Brussels and why you purchased this book.

- **Completing Walks.** Brussels is a compact city. Often a walk begins near where another ends. You can combine walks.

- **Walk the City.** Many destinations are within walking distance of each other. Use a portion of a walk to visit a museum, restaurant or café learning about the city's history along the way.

- **Repetition.** Some topics, such Art Nouveau architecture and the historical development of boulevards, are covered in multiple walks with the assumption not all readers will complete all walks.

- **Debriefing Points.** More Debriefing Points are listed than can be visited by the average visitor. There are also more good ones than can be possibly listed. Stop in any bar or café that looks appealing.

- **Belgian Beer Checklist.** Like traffic signals in Italy, these are suggestions. There are more than 1,500 Belgian beers. The checklist in this book names some 30. Consider them Belgian beers that have faithful followers and that represent different styles. The list focuses on bottled beers, but some Debriefing Points will have a beer on the list as a draft.

- **Beer Types.** Beers are grouped into categories. Try at least one from each. Because Belgian beers are so varied, they are usually listed with their ABV (Alcohol by Volume) number.

- **Flexibility.** Time passes. It is a theme of this book. Cafes will close and streets will be redirected. Look for a new adventure when what appears in the guide has vanished.

Preparing for Brussels

- **Rain.** Bring an umbrella or rain jacket. It rains approximately 200 days a year in Brussels. A sunny day can quickly turn into one with showers – and usually will.

- **Museums.** Every tour book is required to include them, but there are good ones in Brussels. The Brussels Card, which can be purchased in museums, provides free entry to selected museums and unlimited public transport.

- **Public Transportation.** If you do not purchase a Brussels Card, get a 24-hour Jump Ticket at kiosks or ticket windows found in Metro stations and some tram stops. Tickets are valid for Metro, trams and buses.

- **Ordering a Beer.** Ask servers for a beer recommendation or beer of the month. To guide them, be prepared to specify blond or dark beer and high or low alcohol content. Belgian beers range in the low end from 5 to 7% to 10 or 11% ABV. Menus typically list alcohol content with price. "Bieres ou fut" is "beers on draft."

- **Cafes vs Restaurants.** Cafés will serve food or welcome you simply for a drink. Restaurants only offer table service for dining.

- **Café Hours.** Some don't open until 11 AM and others not until 5 PM. If one listed on a walk is closed, choose another that caught your eye.

- **Museum Hours.** Hours vary and most museums are closed on Mondays. Check websites to avoid a disappointment.

Museums on the Walks

Autrique House, Walk 13
(Wed – Sun Noon – 6:00 PM)

AutoWorld, Walk 4
(Mon – Fri 10:00 AM – 5:00 PM; Sat – Sun 10:00 AM – 6:00 PM)

BELvue Museum, Walk 2
(Tue – Fri 9:30 AM – 7:00 PM; Sat – Sun 10:00 AM – 6:00 AM)

Brewers Museum, Walk 12
(Mon – Fri 10:00 AM – 5:00 PM; Sat – Sun 12:00 PM – 5:00 PM)

Cantillon Brewery, Walk 12
(Mon – Sat 10:00 AM – 5:00 PM; closed Wed & Sun)

Chocolate Museum, Walk 12
(Mon – Sun 10:00 AM – 5:00 PM)

Comic Strip Center, Walk 7
(Mon – Sun 10:00 AM – 6:00 PM)

Halle Gate, Walk 9
(Tue – Fri 9:30 AM – 5:00 PM; Sat 10:00 AM – 5:00 PM)

House of European History, Walk 5
(Mon 13:00 – 18:00; Tue – Fri 9:00 AM – 6:00 PM;
 Sat – Sun 10:00 AM – 6:00 PM)

Horta Museum, Walk 8
(Tue – Sun 2:00 PM – 5:30 PM)

Magritte Museum, Walk 3
(Tue – Fri 10:00 AM – 5:00 PM; Sat – Sun 11:00 AM – 6:00 PM)

Museum of City of Brussels, Walk 1
(Tue – Sun 10:00 – 5:00 PM; Thu till 8:00 PM)

Museum of Fantastic Art, Walk 8
(Sat – Sun, May – Sept, 2:00 PM – 5:00 PM)

Museum of Ixelles, Walk 10
(Tue – Sun 9:30 AM – 5:00 PM)

Museum of Original Figurines, Walk 7
(Tue – Sun 10:00 AM – 6:00 PM)

Musical Instruments Museum, Walk 2
(Tue – Fri 9:30 AM – 5:00 PM; Sat – Sun 10:00 AM – 5:00 PM)

Parliamentarium, Walk 5
(Mon 1:00 PM – 6:00 PM; Tue – Fri 9:00 AM – 6:00 PM;
Sat – Sun 10:00 AM – 6:00 PM)

Royal Museum of Central Africa, Walk 14 (To Open in 2018)

Royal Museum of Fine Arts, Walk 3
(Tue – Fri 10:00 AM – 5:00 PM; Sat – Sun 11:00 AM – 6:00 PM)

Royal Museum of Art and History, Walk 4
(Mon – Fri 9:30 AM – 5:00 PM; Sat – Sun 10:00 AM – 5:00 PM)

Royal Museum of the Armed Forces and Military History, Walk 4
(Tue – Sun 9:00 AM – 5:00 PM)

Schaerbeek Museum of Beer, Walk 13
(Wed – Sat 2:00 PM – 6:00 PM)

Temple of Human Passions, Walk 4
(Sat and Sun 10 AM – 4:00 PM March to October)

Tram Museum, Walk 14
(Wed 1:00 PM – 5:00 PM; Sat – Sun 1:00 PM – 7:00 PM)

Wiertz Museum, Walk 5
(Tue – Fri 10:00 AM – 12:00 PM and 12:45 AM – 5:00 PM)

Debriefing Points

A la Mort Subite, Walk 7

A l'Imaige de Notre Dame, Walk 1

Au Bon Vieux, Walk 1

Becasse, Walk 1

Beer Mania, Walk 10

Bier Circus, Walk 13

Bistrot Le Jourdan, Walk 4

Brocanti, Walk 11

Cafe Belga, Walk 10

Cafe Lombard, Walk 1

Chez Bernard, Walk 4

Comic Strip Museum Cafe, Walk 7

De Ultieme Hallucinatie, Walk 13

Delerium, Walk 1

Theatre Royal de Toone, Walk 1

La Fleur en Papier Dore, Walk 3 & 11

La Fontaine, Walk 4

La Porte Noire, Walk 3 & 11

La Porteuse d'Eau, Walk 8

La Terrasse, Walk 4

Le Cirio, Walk 1

Le Chalet Vert, Walk 14

Le Coin Du Diable, Walk 4

Musee des Instruments Café, Walk 2

Maison Antoinne, Walk 4

Moeder Lambic Saint Gilles, Walk 8

Moeder Lambic Fontainas, Walk 12

Monk, Walk 6

Pam Pam at Place du Chatelain, Walk 13

Restobieres, Walk 11

Stam, Walk 10

Ultimeatome, Walk 10

Volle Gas, Walk 10

Beer Check List

Top Fermentation Beers
Yeasts ferment at high temperatures gathering at the tank's top

Flemish Ales (sour with fruit flavors)

Rodenbach Original	6%	Flemish Red Ale
Vanderghinste Oud Bruin	5.5%	Flanders Brown Ale

Dark Ales (spicy and alcoholic)

Kasteel Barista Chocolate Quad	11%	Quadrupel Ale
Chimay Bleue Grande Réserve	9%	Trappist Beer
Westvleteren 12	10.2%	Trappist Beer
Rochefort 10	11.3%	Trappist Beer
Ciney Brune	7%	Dubbel Brown Ale
Val-Dieu Grand Cru	10.5%	Quadrupel Abbey

Blond and Golden Ales (malt sweetness & hop bitterness)

Poperings Hommel	7.5%	Golden Ale
Duvel Tripel Hop	9.5%	Golden Ale
Rulles Estivale	5.2%	Golden Ale
Lupulus	8.5%	Tripel Blond Ale
Barbar	8%	Golden Honey Ale
Tripel Karmeliet	8.4%	Golden Tripel Ale
Achel 8 Blonde	8%	Trappist Beer

Belgian Pale Ales (aromas & flavors of Belgian yeasts & spices)

De Koninck	5%	Amber Ale
Delirium Tremens	9%	Amber Ale
Pauwel Kwak	8.4%	Amber Ale
Bush Ambree	12%	Amber Ale
Troubadour Magma	9%	Tripel Amber Ale
Cuvee de Ranke	7%	Sour Ale
Orval	6.2%	Trappist Beer
Maredsous Blonde	8%	Abbey Beer
Tongerlo 6 Dubbel Blonde	6%	Abbey Beer
De la Senne Brusseleir	8%	Black IPA
Saison Dupont	6.5%	Farmhouse Ale
Saison de St-Feuillien	6.5%	Farmhouse Ale
Avec les Bons Voeux	9.5%	Farmhouse Ale
Silly Sour	5.5%	Farmhouse Ale
Charles Quint Blond	8.5%	Strong Pale Ale

Stouts (roasted oat or barley)

Hercule Stout	9%	Dark Brown Ale
Buffalo Stout	9%	Dark Brown Ale

Wheat Beers (unfiltered & spiced)

La Grande Blanche	7.5%	White Ale
Hoegaarden	4.90%	White Ale

Spontaneous Fermentation Beers

Unfermented wort interacts with yeasts & bacteria in the air

Lambics

Timmermans Lambic Doux	5.5%	Faro
Lindemans Faro	4.2%	Faro
Cantillon Iris	5%	Lambic
Lindemans Kriek	3.5%	Kriek
3 Fonteinen Oude Geuze	6%	Geuze
Lindemans Gueuze Cuvée René	5.5%	Gueuze
Mort Subite Gueuze	4.5%	Gueuze

Bottom Fermentation Beers

Yeasts ferment at low temperatures gathering at the tank's bottom

Lager (smooth, mellow taste)

Cristal	4.8%	Pils
Vedette	5.2%	Pils
Silly Pils	5.0%	Pils

Walk 1
Grand Place

Birthplace of Brussels

Length of Walk:
2.5 hours without museums and debriefs
Museum Options:
Museum of City of Brussels

Connecting Dots: Grand Place and the Lower Town it dominates rest on marshland. Brussels grew to prominence as a commercial center on the Senne River along the trade route connecting Cologne and Bruges. Its standing came from the manufacture of tapestries and other luxury goods of the Middle Ages. As craftsmen and merchants prospered, they constructed guild halls around the main market. By then, the vast expanse of the Lower Town had become a dense mixture of housing, shops and light industry. As years passed, development turned the Senne into an open sewer. To improve public health and beautify the city, the river was covered in the mid-19th Century, destroying much of old Brussels. Taking shape was a new Brussels, molded after great European capitals.

Starting Point: The first stop is Saint Gery Market Hall. To get there, leave the northwest entrance to the Metro at Bourse. That is the entrance on Boulevard Anspach across the street from the Bourse, the large building flanked by lions. Walk south one block along Boulevard Anspach. The spire of City Hall in Grand Place will be on your left. When you reach the point opposite where the Bourse ends, rue J. Van Praet is the street to the right. A street sign high on the corner building reads Place de la Bourse. Turn right onto rue

J. Van Praet. The street will bend slightly to the left. At the intersection of Pont de la Carpe, Saint Gery Market Hall is across the street on your left.

Point 1: Saint Gery Market Hall

If you were standing here at the end of the 6th Century you would be on the largest of three islands, home to a fishing village and an ancient chapel, situated between two arms of the Senne River. It is considered the original center of Brussels. In 979, a fortress was built here to serve as a trading post, entering the settlement into the writings of history. Brussels, a derivation of the Dutch name for marshland, "Broussella," was born.

By the 12th Century, Brussels was an important point on the trade route connecting Bruges and Ghent to Cologne. The Flemish cities were among the richest in Medieval Northern Europe largely due to the production of lace. Brussels' contribution was the manufacture of tapestries and the work of goldsmiths and silversmiths who plied their skills on the precious metals transported from Cologne. To

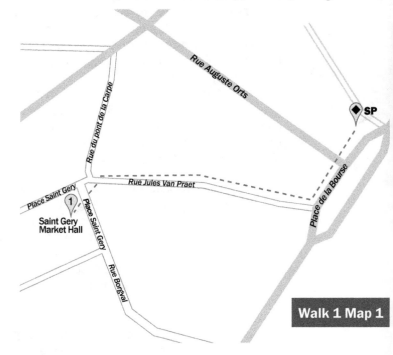

protect Brussels' strategic importance on this luxury trade route of the Middle Ages, the Duchy of Brabant, a kingdom covering modern day Belgium and parts of the Netherlands, established a court in Brussels.

In the 13th Century, the Duchy constructed a wall encircling the city which at the time included the islands, markets, a sea port, Saint-Michael-and-Gudula church, and settlements at the top of the hill to the east. To escape the crowded conditions of the Lower Town, the duke's court moved to a new palace built as a part of the new fortification on the eastern hill. As centuries passed, the First Wall of Brussels slowly integrated into the urban structure.

Today, the ancient site of Brussels' founding is home to the Saint-Gery Market. Walk into the hall. Originally an open-air market, the current building dates from 1881 when it was built in the Neo-Romantic style featuring the new building materials of the 19th Century: Cast iron and glass. Large sections of the surrounding area were demolished to be replaced by bourgeoisie housing and shops. The city scape you are in today characterizes what you would have seen in the sections of other European capitals built in the late 19th Century.

Exit at the opposite end of the market onto rue de la Grande Ile. Turn left.

Point 2: Au Lion d'Or

Immediately to the right is a building dating from 1811 that stands in the place of a 17th Century inn, Au Lion d'Or. You can enter the grounds through the arched entrance to the former carriage house.

During renovations to turn the building into an apartment house, a branch of the Senne River was uncovered. The building spans it. This is the only place in Brussels where the river that once flowed openly in Brussels can be seen. Ruins of the old brewery and bakery of the long-gone Riches Claires Convent as well as quays that served local businesses were also uncovered.

This is a tranquil escape from the hustle and bustle of modern day Brussels.

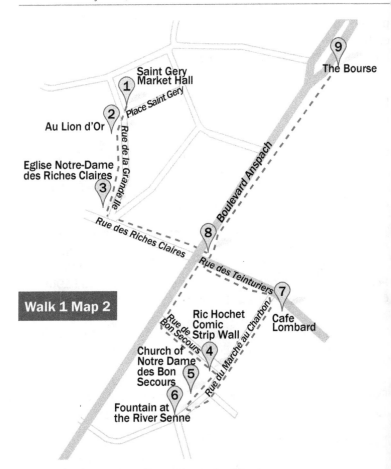

Point 3: Eglise Notre-Dame des Riches Claires

Continue for another block along rue de la Grande Ile, going away from Saint Gery's Market Hall.

The Order of Poor Ladies, officially the Order of Saint Clare, was founded by Saints Clare of Assisi and Francis of Assisi in 1212. In the 14th Century, the order founded a convent to the south near Porte de Halle. After it was burned by beggars in 1558, the nuns moved to a convent abandoned by the Sisters of Nazareth at this location.

From 1665 to 1670 a Flemish Renaissance style chapel, Notre Dame aux Riches Claires, was built for the nuns. As was the mission of their order, the nuns provided free education to the children of the poor.

In 1796, because of the French Revolution, the Poor Clares were evicted from their convent. The church became a military store. The other monastic buildings were sold in 1805 as national property. The streets 'St. Christopher' and 'Riches-Claires' were drawn through the monastery property. The church escaped destruction becoming a parish in 1806. Its shape today is the result of a nave built in 1824 on the left side and one on the right added in 1833.

Continue along rue de la Grande Ile, walking past rue de la St. Gery and turning immediately left away from the church at the intersection with rue de Riches Claires. Cross Boulevard Anspach, turning right and walking one block along the boulevard to rue du Bon Secours. Go left.

Point 4: Ric Hochet Comic Strip Wall

On the wall in front of you is a fresco featuring the comic book character Ric Hochet. A journalist who drives a Porsche from crime scene to crime scene, Ric displays here his athletic skills as a criminal lurks in the background.

Belgium is the homeland of many great comic book artists, including the creators of Tintin, The Smurfs, and Mortimer to name a few. Ric Hochet was the work of Tibet, the pseudonym of strip's artist, and A.P. Duchâteau, the scenario writer.

Before turning right onto rue du Marche au Charbon, look back down rue Bon Secours. You will see a noticeable change in elevation. When the Senne was covered at the end of the 19th Century, the river was diverted underground through two channels. The one meter difference shows where the channels were added. Residents of the time referred to these differences in street height as "Anspach bumps," named after the mayor of Brussels during the time of the works.

Point 5: Church of Notre Dame de Bon Secours

Just one block to the right on rue du Marché au Charbon is the Church of Notre Dame de Bon Secours. Founded in the 12th Century on the site of an inn that welcomed visitors to Brussels, the small chapel was totally transformed in 1625 when a shoemaker found what was believed to be a miraculous statue. To accommodate the influx of visitors the church was expanded.

The church's Italianate-Flemish style took the shape we see today after the bombardment of 1695 and renovations in the 19th and 20th Centuries.

Point 6: Fountain at the River Senne

To the left of the church at the intersection of rue du Jardin des Olives, two small fountains are a reminder that the Senne River flowed next to the church until the end of the 19th Century.

Resting within a confined space, the Lower Town of Medieval Brussels was characterized by dense housing. Wooden additions to buildings hung over the river.

With its undependable river flow, the Senne had never been particularly good for navigation. Unregulated development made matters worse. Haphazardly constructed bridges impeded river traffic. During heavy rains, the river and the waste which was dumped into it flooded houses and shops. Periodic epidemics swept the city.

In the 16th Century the first of Brussels' canals were built, ending navigation on the Senne. By the 17th Century, the Senne was more open sewer than river, no longer having a commercial purpose. In the 19th Century, it was diverted into tunnels and covered.

Retrace your steps on rue du Marché au Charbon heading north and passing rue du Bon Secours.

Point 7: Cafe Lombard

Before ducking into Café Lombard at the corner of rue du Lombard for a debrief, check out two more comic strip murals.

In front of you, Broussaille, the blond figure, and his girlfriend Catherine walk through the streets of Brussels. Painted by Frank Pé in 1991, it was Brussels' first giant comic mural. In 1999, Catherine was repainted to add a more feminine hairstyle, earrings and if you look closely bigger breasts. The mural gives a nod to the city's gay community centered in the neighborhood.

On the wall behind you, Victor Sackville, a spy in the service of His Majesty during the First World War, moves around Brussels while fulfilling a secret mission. Francis Carin is the artist.

Café Lombard is on the list of Debriefing Points because it offers a wide selection of Belgian beers on draft. Hopefull, Silly pils with its aroma of barley and hops will be one of them. Another choice is the Silly Sour, a blend of 13% of traditional dark saison with the remainder 87% soured ale.

Now is a good place to learn about the vaulting of the Senne.

Prior to this 19th Century project, Brussels looked as Brugge does today: A city of waterways and small alleys.

In the 1860s, Mayor Jules Anspach conceived of a plan to rid the city of epidemics and to beautify it in the mold of Paris. Anspach also hoped to increase the city's tax base by luring the wealthy businessmen and merchants living in the suburbs into the city center. Fueled by the mining of iron ore and coal and a manufacturing base that produced the railroads of Europe, Belgium boasted one of the world's largest economies. Its financial center was Brussels.

To implement his vision, Anspach called upon a law passed earlier by the Belgian Parliament allowing government to expropriate privately owned land for the "greater good." For the Senne project, the city confiscated large swaths of land, far more than what was needed, as a means of financing the project. The city's plan was to resell the land at a profit to speculators who would build upscale stores and housing on the newly created grandiose boulevards.

The project did not start smoothly. Leading engineers believed that because of Brussels' geology the tunnels would accumulate potentially dangerous gases and would not be able to handle enough water to prevent floods. City activists objected to the high cost, what they considered poor compensation for seized property, and the lack of public input into the project. Even though the river was a risk to public health, the housing surrounding it was home to thousands of poor residents who would be now be forced to cram into other districts that were already crowded.

Anspach awarded the project to a private British company especially created for the task. The contract was signed on June 15, 1866, and the expropriation of the first 1,100 houses was completed a few months later. Excavation began on February 13, 1867. Partway through construction the private company was forced to relinquish control of the project to the city because one of its directors alleg-edly attempted to steal 2.5 million francs from the company. The scandal and geological issues delayed the project's completion until 1871.

Excluding the sewers built upriver and downriver in adjacent suburbs, the covered section was to be 2.2 kilometers (1.4 miles) in length. Constructed with bricks, the covering consisted of two parallel 6 meter (20 feet) wide tunnels and a set of two lateral drainage pipes, each taking in waste water from its respective side of the street.

Return to Boulevard Anspach by walking down rue des Teinturiers. But before leaving, male readers should visit the washroom to observe massive English urinals.

Point 8: Boulevard Anspach

Turn right on Boulevard Anspach, heading north.

Boulevard Anspach, then known as Central Boulevard, was the most prominent of the avenues to come from the vaulting of the Senne. Their opening improved access to the Lower Town and facilitated traffic flow from and to the north and south train stations. To stimulate the revitalization of the Lower Town, public buildings such as the Bourse, where you will visit next, were constructed.

Realizing private buildings on the boulevards and surrounding streets presented a greater challenge. Development was slow. High land prices limited the number of people who could afford to live here. Those who could generally preferred living in new suburbs rather than in apartments in the cramped quarters of the city center. In the suburbs, families enjoyed nearby parks and gardens, where homes were designed each with their own character to distinguish them from those of neighbors and to illustrate their owners' success.

The vaulting of the Senne changed Brussels forever. Today, the boulevards in the center city are characterized by classic urban architecture from the end of the 19th Century. It is hard to imagine that a river flowed on the exact place where cars and pedestrians pass along Boulevard Anspach today.

Point 9: The Bourse

After walking several blocks, you will see a large Neo-Renaissance building guarded by lions. It was the home of the Brussels stock exchange. Designed as the focal point of a new business district amid the complex of 19th Century buildings that arose over the Senne, it was constructed on the site of the old butter market which itself had been built on the remains of an ancient convent.

High above the entrance is a pediment entitled "Belgium Teaching Commercial and Industrial Expansion." Supported by six Doric columns, it is decorated by a female relief representing the City of Brussels with two figures on either side of her symbolizing trade and industry. Beneath the pediment are two winged statues representing Good and Evil. Works by Rodin can also be found in the building's decoration. With stocks on the Brussels stock exchange now traded on computers, the building is "dead" except for hosting occasional exhibits.

Walk past the Bourse and turn right onto rue de Bourse. A glass enclosure with ruins below will be on your right.

Point 10: Ruins of Recollets Convent

In 1238, the Recollets Franciscan convent was established here, close to the Senne River and Saint Nicolas church which will you visit in a few stops. The convent was dissolved in the religious wars of the 16th Century, and the building was severely damaged during the bombardment of 1695. The ruins were discovered during renovations to the Bourse in 1988. Numerous tombs, including the tomb of Jean I, Duke of Brabant, who died in 1294, have been unearthed here.

Point 11: Cirio

Immediately on your left at No. 18 is Le Cirio, called the most beautiful brasserie in Brussels. Often crowded and known for its Art Nouveau toilets as much as its beer list, Le Ciro is worth a quick look inside. The name dates from the late 1800s when an Italian inventor of a tomato-canning process opened restaurants and delicatessens in major European cities. The Brussels store is one of the few remaining. It is easy to imagine stock brokers leaving the Bourse to take a break at Cirio for a "half and half," its signature drink of Champaign and white wine.

Walk to the end of the street. Turn left on rue du Midi to find a debriefing point. Look for the neon arrow "Becasse" pointing to an alley a few steps away.

Point 12: A la Becasse

La Becasse, woodcock in French, at 11 rue Tabora is listed as a Debriefing Point because it serves Timmermans Lambic Doux in the traditional way, in a ceramic mug by waiters wearing monk-like aprons.

Lambic beer is made from 60% malted barley and 40% wheat and is brewed with aged hops. What sets lambics apart from other beers is spontaneous fermentation brewing. With lambics, the liquid wort extracted from the mashing process of the grains ferments over several months through interaction with the wild yeasts in the outside air. Next comes one to three years of aging in wooden casks. The result is an acidic beer typical of what was served in the Senne River Valley for centuries prior to the advent of the steam engine and the mechanical refrigeration technology that revolutionized brewing.

Point 13: Saint Nicholas Church

Retrace your steps along rue du Midi and stop in front of the church. Just steps away from Medieval markets, the church is appropriately named for Saint Nicholas, the patron saint of merchants. Established in the 11th Century, the church lays claim to being Brussels' oldest. It is one of the few standing reminders of the city's Medieval past even though the church has been severely damaged several times over the centuries including during the French bombardment in 1695. A cannonball is still lodged in one of the pillars. Renovations have obscured much of the Romanesque character of the original church. The Gothic-style houses and shops that form the church's west facade were built in 1956 along rue du Midi and in fact hold the building up.

Walk along the right side of the church along Petite rue au Beurre to rue Marche-aux-Herbes. You are standing directly behind the church.

Point 14: Impasse for Au Bon Vieux

Across from St. Nicholas Church is Au Bon Vieux. Look for the sign and peer into the small doorway beneath it to see a small alley. A few doors away to the left is another passageway. It leads to A l'Imaige de Notre Dame.

These bars opened in the 1880s. The houses date from the late 17th Century.

At Au Bon Vieux you can enjoy a Westvleteren abbey ale. Westvleteren is said to produce the best beer in the world. The price reflects that, although that might also be due to the beer being brewed in such small quantities it can only be purchased from the doors of the monastery to individual buyers holding reservations. The bottle has no label so the server will present the cap to you after the beer is poured to assure you that you will be drinking a genuine Westvleteren.

Medieval Brussels, with its cramped living conditions, was full of little passages and alleys like the ones leading to Au Bon Vieux and A l'Imaige de Notre Dame. Some were dead ends while others led to stalls of merchants grouped into markets. Dangerous and disease ridden during Medieval times, the walkways that remain preserve the memory of a long-ago time through their names: Marche-aux-Herbes (herbs), Au Buerre (butter), Bouchers (butchers), Fromage (cheese) and Poulets (chicken).

Return to rue March-aux-Herbes heading away from Boulevard Anspach. Make the first left onto rue de la Fourche. The first street to the right (not counting a small alley) is rue des Bouchers. Turn onto it.

Immediately to your left is Impasse de la Fidelite.

Point 15: Delerium

Midway down on the left is Delirium, a tourist mecca that holds the Guinness Book of Records for largest beer selection, more than 2,000. There is no better place than here to have a Delirium Tremens from the Huyghe's Brewery near Ghent. DT is made with three different yeasts to create a beer in which the alcohol warms the tongue as it is drunk. Consider following a DT with Kasteel Barista Chocolate Quad. It is a strong one at 11% ABV with aromas of chocolate, coffee, dried fruits and toffee. Want a real chocolate flavored beer? Ask for the Floris Chocolat also from Brouwerij Huyghetry. This is a Belgian fruit beer, not a favorite among serious beer drinkers but one that has a following none the less.

Across the passageway is Jeanneke-Pis, the female Mannekin Pis. The little peeing boy is not on any walk in this guide, but when you visit the Grand Place, the guide will point you in the right direction if your tourist instincts cannot be submerged.

Return to rue des Bouchers, continuing to the left until you enter a covered walkway. Columns stand on each side of the entrance.

Point 16: Galeries Royales Saint-Hubert

You are at the midpoint of the Galeries Royales Saint-Hubert, an Italian Renaissance styled structure built in 1846. It predates the other glass enclosed arcades that became popular in mid-19th Century Europe.

Turn right.

The impetus behind the construction was a recurring theme in 19th Century Brussels. The city fathers and the Belgian king wanted the capital of Belgium to have the stature of other major European cities. The galleries swept away dimly lit and dangerous alleys like those you just walked through, replacing them with a protected shopping experience featuring fine boutiques and brasseries. A sign at the entrance welcomed visitors with the Latin words "Omnibus omnia" (Everything for everybody).

Like in other European arcades, a theater was located inside. Théâtre des Galeries Saint-Hubert opened June 7, 1847, becoming one of three royal theaters in Brussels, playing operetta and revues.

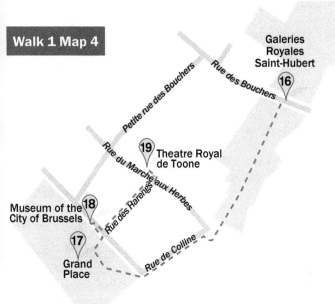

Walk 1 Map 4

Galeries
Royales
Saint-Hubert
16

Rue des Bouchers

Petite rue des Bouchers

Rue du Marché aux Herbes

19 Theatre Royal
de Toone

Rue des Harengs

Museum of the 18
City of Brussels

17

Rue de Colline

Grand
Place

It figured prominently in film history, when on March 1, 1896, it showcased a Lumière Brothers' cinematograph. This was only two months after the brothers held the first public viewing of their invention in Paris. The Lumières transformed the theater into a permanent venue for the showing of their films, creating the first "cinema" in Belgium.

Looking down the arcade, you will see that it bends. This is by design, adding the perspective of length and breaking the tedium of columns, windows and arches. For a chocolate treat within the gallery, you have many choices: Mary's Chocolates, Le Chocolat, L'or Noir des Bruxellois, or the original Neuhaus.

Neuhaus, which began in 1857, contributed to the reputation of Belgium chocolates with its 1912 creation of the chocolate bonbon or praline, the creamy candies covered in a chocolate shell. To protect the pralines from being crushed by the customary paper wrapping, the company invented the chocolate gift box in 1915.

You are heading south in the direction of Grand Place. After exiting the galleries, cross rue Marche aux Herbes and walk down rue de Colline. Head for the spire.

Point 17: Grand Place

Originally an open space on dried up marsh near the markets and old port, Grand Place lay on the causeway linking the Rhineland to Flanders. In the 11th Century residences constructed of thatch and timber began to appear followed by the establishment of a small royal court of the Brabants, a state of the Holy Roman Empire.

Merchants came next, arriving in growing numbers to service the court and the surrounding population, eventually opening stalls that lined the streets, haphazardly built in all directions. The streets took on the names of the goods that were sold there. To provide a surface for merchants to more easily move their goods and on which to erect their stalls, residents collected pebbles from the Senne River and laid them on the ground to create pavements.

At the beginning of the 14th Century, the Duke of Brabant built enclosed markets to sell meat, bread and cloth. Not only did this allow the markets to be open in bad weather, it also provided for storage and improved control of inventory, enabling the duke to more accurately account for sales taxes.

With the population of Brussels at around 30,000, the 14th Century saw the emergence of influence by merchants and tradesman. To raise money for the expansion of the castle in the Upper Town, the Duke of Brabant sold his cloth mills and other businesses around in the Lower Town to local authorities. They went to work relieving congestion by demolishing buildings and defining the outline of today's Grand Place square, creating a suitable place for tournaments and executions, both of which would draw customers.

Focus your attention on the building with the tall spire, Hotel de Ville.

In the 15th Century, Brussels was a rich and powerful city, the beneficiary of wealth from the cloth trade. The city required a home for its administrative offices to showcase its importance. Residences were cleared, and in 1401 the foundation was laid for what would be a grand Gothic style city hall.

Hotel de Ville, or city hall, is the tallest building in the square. The archangel St. Michael, the patron saint of Brussels, caps its spire. Look carefully and you will notice the tower and entrance arch are not centered. Legend says that when the architect discovered his error he leapt to his death from the tower. Truth be told, the design was intentional to increase the thickness of the right-hand wall to provide adequate support for the tower. Before Belgium gained its independence in 1830, the rulers of lands surrounding Brussels were enthroned in the city hall. The statues that for years adorned the front of the building are now displayed in the Museum of the City of Brussels across the square.

Not to be outdone when city officials built the city hall, the duke, even though he and the other nobles had long been safely ensconced in the Upper Town, began construction of his own symbol of authority across from city hall. In 1504, he opened Maison du Roi, or King's House, on the site of the old covered bread market. The bakers had abandoned their market preferring to sell their goods door to door. No king or duke ever lived in the building.

At the corner of the square to the left of the King's House is Le Roy d'Espagna pub.

Originally the Bakers' guild house, Le Roy d'Espagna has a bust of Charles II on its facade, giving the house its name. Charles II was King of Spain when the house was built in 1697, the time when the lands of today's Belgium were a Spanish conquest. Inside is a stuffed horse and ceilings with animal blatters. From the second floor, visitors can sit in romantic alcoves with a view of the Grand Place. When Brussels is cold and wet, a place next to a roaring fire on the ground floor is a prime location. The terrace outside is an attraction on sunny days.

As the population and commerce grew in the 14th and 15th Centuries, merchants and craftsmen prospered, forming guilds, like the Baker's Guild, to further their businesses. They displayed their prosperity in grand halls constructed around the Grand Place where they held meetings and complained about the duke's regulations and taxes.

Originally, the term "guild" was reserved for those in the cloth trade. It was not until the 14th Century when other trades were afforded use of the term. Guilds set standards, regulated working conditions and salaries, provided training and established prices and commercial terms. By the 16th Century, there were 59 craft guilds in Brussels. The guilds also offered the structure by which businesses interacted with the city government and the dukes.

The original guild halls were made of wood, but the magnificent Grand Place of today owes much to the French bombardment of Brussels in 1695 and the resulting fire that destroyed the halls and 4,000 other buildings, a third of the city, leaving not much more than the Town Hall's tower standing.

As a statement to the wealth and power of the guilds, within 5 years, the halls were rebuilt, this time in a Baroque style under orders from the city magistrate with reliefs or gold details representing the respective trades or important events in city history.

Start at Le Roy d'Espagna and begin walking around the square in a counter clockwise direction. Standing in front of each building, look for the decorative features.

At the Bakers Guild, Nos. 1-2, now Le Roi d'Espagne, statues represent the six ingredients of bread: energy, agriculture, wind, fire, water and prudence. The Tallow Dealers (the meat fat used to make candles and soap) conducted their business at No. 3. Above the door at No. 4 Le Sac, one worker holds a sack while another removes its contents. This was the house of the Joiners and Coopers, cabinet makers and barrel makers.

Romulus and Remus being suckled by a wolf greet you at No. 5 La Louve (the She Wolf), home of the Archers. On top, a golden phoenix rises from the ashes, a symbol of the square's rebirth after the French bombardment. The Boat Makers had their hall Le Cornet (The Horn) at No. 6. The lower levels show nautical symbols and the top level replicates the stern of a frigate. A wooden statue of a fox is at No. 7 den Vos, the Mercers. These merchants traded in fine fabrics and were employed as haberdashers and shirt makers.

Move around the corner past the Hotel de Ville.

The house originally standing at No. 8 named L'Etoile (The Star) is mentioned as early as the 13th Century in the city's historical documents. Destroyed in the bombardment of 1695 and rebuilt, it was demolished again in 1852 when roads entering Grand Place were widened. In 1897, Mayor Charles Buls renovated the City Hall and reconstructed No. 8, including space for trams to enter Grand Place.

On the house's side, a plaque depicts the deathbed scene of Everard 't Serclaes, a 14th Century burgomaster who died at No. 8 in 1388 from injuries that included his tongue being torn out and right foot cut off by men enlisted by a Brabant baron to settle a score over the purchase of adjoining lands.

Serclaes came to prominence when he led a surprise night assault on the city walls in 1356 to free the city from the rule of the Count of Flanders, earning him the title Savior of Brussels. The three bas-reliefs recount two episodes in the history of Brussels in which Everard 't Serclaes was a central figure. Shortly after the statue's unveiling in 1905, a legend developed that those who rubbed the statue could have a wish fulfilled or would have good luck.

If you are compelled to visit Manneken Pis, you will find him perhaps in a colorful costume amid admiring tourists a few blocks away down rue Charles Buls. Another peeing statute, Het Zinnek, the pissing dog, relieves himself at the corner of Rue des Chartreux and Rue de Vieux-Marche, a few blocks from the Saint Gery Market Hall.

Back to the guild halls. No. 9 is Le Cygne (The Swan), the Butchers' headquarters. A white swan sits atop the entry to a current day restaurant. The Brewers held sway at No. 10 L'Arbre d'Or (The Golden Tree) topped by an equestrian statue of Charles of Lorraine, a patron of local brewers. Long standing private homes are at Nos. 11 and 12.

Along the eastern side of the square, the façade is a string of seven houses known as the House of the Dukes of Brabant built after the French bombardment for administrative purposes. Under the first-floor windows are the busts of nineteen Dukes of Brabant.

Nos. 13 and 14 are named for Fame and Crayfish, respectively; No. 15 is the former Tanners Guild; No. 16 the Millers; No. 17 the Carpenters; No. 18 the Stonemasons. No. 19 is named La Bourse for trade.

To complete the tour, move around the northeast corner.

Cerf (the Deer) marks a private house that once belonged to the architect Gilles Van de Eynde. The next buildings are named Anne and Joseph at No. 20 and Nos. 21-22, respectively. No. 23, L'Ange (the Angel), built in 1697 in the Italian Flemish style, is the building with Doric and Ionic pilasters.

The former Maison des Tailleurs (House of the Tailors) is at No. 24-25 La Chaloupe d'Or (the Golden Sloop or Lifeboat). The Tailor's patroness, St. Barbara, peers out from above the doorway. Moving to the top of the building, St. Boniface, a native of Brussels, blesses visitors to the square below.

At No. 26-27 Le Pigeon (the Pigeon) the Painters sat. In the 1850s, Victor Hugo lived here in exile from France until the city asked him to leave to not draw wrath of Napoleon II on the city.

Crossing rue des Harengs, you arrive at the final segment. No. 28 is Le Marchand d'Or, named in honor of a gold merchant who once lived there. The building dates from 1709, but the spot has long been known as La Chambrette de l'Amman (the Little Chamber of the Amman). The name refers to a city position that during reign of the Brabants carried out the will of the duke in administrative matters. The amman is said to have lived at No. 8 in the 13th Century, perhaps moving to No. 28 sometime later. The Duchy of Brabant's coat of arms adorns the front of the building.

Cross over rue au Beurre to view Nos. 39 to 34. From left to right, they are L'Ane (The Donkey), Ste-Barbe (St. Barbara), Le Chêne (The Oak Tree), Le Peitit Renard (The Little Fox), Le Paon (The Peacock), and Le Heaume (The Helmet).

Point 18: Museum of the City of Brussels

Return to The King's House across from city hall to visit the city museum. Since its construction early in the 16th Century, the King's House has taken on many shapes. The current building dates from the 1800s. Maps, displays and paintings on the second floor track the development of Brussels.

The third floor displays 100 costumes that have been worn by Manneken Pis. The little boy's entire wardrobe totals more than 900 outfits. A city employee changes them on a prescribed schedule of 23 fixed dates and to commemorate newsworthy events.

After leaving, walk down the street to right of The King's House, rue des Harengs. Directly across at rue du Marché aux Herbes 66 is a Debriefing Point.

Point 19: Theatre Royal de Toone

Theatre Royal de Toone is at the end of Impasse Schuddeveld, an alley running from the Petite rue des Bouchers and another alley running off rue du Marché aux Herbes. As its name implies, marionette shows – most often in the Bruxellois dialect but at times in English – are held here. The theater has operated in different premises since 1830 under the leadership of a puppet master designated as Toone. The current master is Toone VIII, who assumed the title from this father, Toone VII in 2003.

The theater serves beers in a café apart from the performances. A favorite here is Pauwel Kwak, a Belgian strong pale ale served in a traditional glass. In the 18th Century, a well-known Belgian brewer, Pauwel Kwak had a coaching inn on the road between Mechelen and Gent. In those days, the Napoleonic Code ruled that coach drivers were forbidden to drink beer with their passengers meaning they were not allowed to leave the coach to quench their thirst. Pauwel Kwak invented an efficient solution to this problem by offering his beer in a special glass that could be fixed to the carriage.

Return: It is a short but perhaps unsteady walk back to the Metro at the Bourse or the stop at Central Station.

Walk 2
Upper Town

The Royal Grounds

Length of Walk: 1.5 hours without museums or debriefs
Museum Options: BELvue Museum • Musical Instruments Museum

Connecting Dots: About 1100, the rulers of the region that included Brussels constructed a castle on a hill overlooking the marshland and settlements along the Senne River. The castle was incorporated into the First Wall that encircled Brussels. Since then, the Upper Town has been a center of royal power, home to the rulers of lands around Brussels and connected to royal families in other cities. To accommodate an expanding city, a Second Wall was built to widen the circle of fortification, enclosing the castle. As was only fitting for a city that as part of the Holy Roman Empire had amassed wealth and power, the castle evolved into a magnificent palace.

In the early 19th Century, Brussels was not spared the social unrest that overtook much of Europe. In 1830, revolution achieved separation from the Netherlands. After adopting a national constitution in 1831, the new Belgian Parliament invited Leopold I, a German noble, to be the country's king. In the royal setting of the Upper Town, Leopold I swore to uphold the constitution's liberal tenants, introducing an era of prosperity.

Leopold II, after inheriting the throne from his father, used the country's wealth and his personal fortune from ownership of an African colony to transform Brussels into a major European capital, building grand boulevards and parks, sometimes over the objections of local politicians and the general population. Among Leopold II's first projects was to expand the Royal Palace.

Starting Point: Entrance to Metro at Parc.

Point 1: Parc de Bruxelles

Exit the Metro and turn right to walk into the park following the path along the fence bordering rue de la Loi.

In an area known for its rolling hills and meandering streams, a 14th Century duke built walls to enclose a large portion of the land near Coudenberg Castle as a royal retreat. Later dukes stocked game, added cages for exotic birds, built gardens with fountains, and arranged jousting tournaments.

In 1775, the Dutch government gave approval to create a public park with strolling paths on the former preserve. The ground was leveled, trees planted and roads traced in a geometric plan. When looking from above, the design of the Masonic protractor can be seen with its head at the north end of the park and its legs extending to the corners of the southern end.

Stop at the main path cutting through the center of the park. The Belgian Parliament building stands across rue de la Loi. At the park's other end, directly opposite, sits the Royal Palace, a symbolic reference that the power of Parliament equaled that of the king.

Walk into the park along this central path, circling a pond built in 1855. You will come to an octagonal basin built in 1780 surrounded by eight statues to Hermes. Further along on the right is a grandstand. Built in 1841, it displays the names of 12 famous musicians.

Continue walking south, towards the Royal Palace. Stop when you reach the street.

Point 2: Royal Palace

The Royal Palace is a monument to the reign of Leopold II, Belgium's builder king.

Leopold II assumed the throne as Belgium's second king in 1865 upon the death of his father. He immediately embarked on a master plan to mold Brussels into a grand European capital, beginning with expanding the modest palace built at the end of the 18th Century that served the needs of his father and the Dutch king before him. The palace quickly doubled in size.

The Royal Palace is not a residence. Since 1936, the royal family has resided on the outskirts of the city in Laeken. The Royal Palace is where the royal family welcomes foreign officials and members of the Belgian Parliament. If the Belgian flag waves above the palace, the king is in the country. Rue Royale, which passes on the western side of the Royal Park, connects the Palace of Justice to the south, runs through the Place Royale, past the Royal Park, and terminates at the Royal Residence in Laeken, giving it the name Royal Route.

Leopold II's legacy is largely associated with the Belgian Congo. Leopold II believed all great countries had colonies, and he looked to Africa and Asia to secure one for Belgium. Being rebuffed by the Belgian Parliament did not deter him. He formed a private holding company disguised as a scientific and philanthropic association and hired the journalist and explorer Henry Morton Stanley to chart the Congo region of Africa and negotiate with local tribal leaders. At the Berlin Conference of 1884-85, later called the "Scramble for Africa," King Leopold's company was awarded the area that Stanley had explored introducing Western civilization and Christianity.

Seventy-six times the size of Belgium and controlled by Leopold's private army, the Free Congo State enabled Leopold to amass a vast personal fortune through the sale of ivory and harvesting of rubber. After it became known how poorly the Congolese were treated, the international community forced Leopold II to cede the colony to the Belgian government in 1908. By then the Builder King had become widely unpopular. When he died in 1909, crowds booed his funeral cortege as it wended its way through Brussels. As a final insult, his marriage five days before his death to a prostitute with whom he had two illegitimate children was declared by Parliament to have no legal standing.

The Congo remained a colony of Belgium until it was granted independence in 1960, the result of wide-spread popular unrest and pressure from the United States.

Point 3: BELvue Museum

Turn right upon exiting the park, crossing the street at the crosswalk to be on the same side as the Royal Palace. The building to the right of the palace at the corner houses the BELvue Museum.

The building opened in 1776 as the Belle-Vue Hotel to cater to the moneyed classes, mainly from England, who came to visit Brussels. In 1830 the hotel took center stage in the fight for Belgian independence.

As in the rest of Europe, social unrest among the lower classes began to brew in the first decades of the 19th Century. After a patriotic opera was presented at a theater in the Lower Town, a crowd gathered in the park across the street from the Royal Palace to protest working conditions.

The crowd became violent. Royal troops took refuge in the Belle-Vue Hotel from where they then fired into the crowd. Protests swept the country. After local militia forced the retreat of the Dutch Army from Brussels, Southern Netherlands (today's Belgium) declared independence from Northern Netherlands. A parliament was elected a month later, and in 1831 it adopted a constitution that protected the interests of the rich and guaranteed basic rights of speech, press, religion and language.

The museum tells the story of Belgian independence, describes how the country promoted its industrial prowess through international exhibitions, portrays popular and not so popular monarchs, and reflects the optimism of post-World War II Belgium culminating with the country's hosting of the 1958 World's Fair.

Exit the museum turning left to rue Royale where you turn left again to enter a square.

Point 4: Place Royale

Place Royale, a symmetrical square constructed in Viennese Neo-Classical style, lies in the center of the Upper Town. At its heart stands the equestrian statue of Godefroid de Bouillon, leader of the first crusade. In the 19th Century, the square was a commercial center, the location of upscale cafes, shops and hotels such as the Belle-Vue.

Dominating the square is the columned St. Jacob of the Coudenberg Church, the place where on July 21, 1831, the German duke selected by Belgium's Parliament to be Belgium's king as Leopold I swore allegiance to the country's constitution.

When the Belgians came courting, Leopold had already turned down the job of being Greece's king following the Greek War of Independence, considering the government there unstable. Belgium, unlike the Greeks, had a quick war of independence and a constitution. He could tell they meant business getting their new state up and running. The Belgian's liked Leopold because of his diplomatic relationships with European heads of state and especially the perception of his being favored by the United Kingdom, a useful counterweight should France press territorial claims against its new neighbor to the east.

Walk 2 Map 2

Cross rue Royale stopping at the northwest corner of the square.

Point 5: Ruins of Coudenberg Castle

Peak through basement windows of the building on the corner. Exposed are archeological ruins of Coudenberg Castle, the place where nobles of the Duchy of Brabant held court from the 14th to 18th Centuries.

Coudenberg Castle was constructed as a part of the First Wall surrounding Brussels around 1100. The heights of Coudenberg Hill allowed the nobles to dominate the Lower Town and escape the outbreaks of disease that periodically decimated the population living near the Senne River.

By the 13th Century, the land that today includes Belgium was consolidated as the Duchy of Brabant, part of the Holy Roman

Empire. Coudenberg Castle was one of its important seats of power, along with castles in Antwerp and Leuven.

After the city was invaded by the King of Flanders during a succession crisis in the 1350s, it became evident stronger fortifications were needed. A new wall was built enclosing a larger area, allowing Coudenberg Castle to be transformed from a military outpost to a residential palace. By then the Duchy had passed into the hands of Burgundian nobles. By the late 1400s, the Duchy had become part of the Spanish branch of the Hapsburg Dynasty. Later, the Austrian Hapsburgs ruled the city and region.

By 1500, Coudenberg had been vastly expanded to include banquet halls for pageants and chambers for councils of the Duchy's rulers and clergy. The square outside was the site of markets, festivals and executions. Those who sought the favor of the royals built elegant mansions in the area and relaxed in the castle's garden, today the Royal Park.

Everything changed in February 1731 when a fire broke out in the palace's kitchen. The entire building became engulfed in fames. Freezing conditions made it impossible to deliver water and an attempt to use beer to extinguish the flames was not successful (and was short lived). The palace lay in ruins until 1774 when redevelopment began, resulting in the construction of Place Royale and the original building for today's Royal Palace.

Follow the sidewalk that hugs the buildings. Cross Montagne de la Cour, the street that enters the square from the west and winds down to the Lower Town becoming Coudenberg. After crossing the street, start walking down the hill.

Point 6: Musical Instruments Museum

The building across the street on the right is Old England, a former department store and now the home of the Musical Instruments Museum. It stands as a classic example of Art Nouveau architecture. If you wish to visit, wait until you finish the rest of the walk when you can return on the same side of the street as the museum.

After the turn of the 19th Century, the area surrounding the newly built Place Royale became home to the type of fashionable shops that dotted the urban landscapes of Europe. Old England sold luxury goods to the nobles and wealthy residents of the townhomes near the palace as well as to English tourists passing through on their way to visiting the Battlefield of Waterloo where Napoleon was defeated in 1815. Waterloo is 13 kilometers (8 miles) to the southeast.

Old England began operating in Brussels in 1886. The building we see today was built on a vacant lot as its new home between 1898 and 1900, a design of Brussels architect Paul Saintenoy. Housed within Old England's delicate metal façade, merchants operated out of small shops selling clothes for men, women and children and also toys, perfumes, haberdashery, clocks, stationery, sports and garden supplies. Old England was a true department store. In the early 1900s, the store acquired several adjoining buildings to expand.

Walk a little further down the hill stopping in the open area near a fountain and pond.

Point 7: Delacre Pharmacy and Hotel Ravenstein

Saintnoy also designed the building to the left of Old England. Built in 1895 in the Flemish Renaissance style, its façade was meant to recapture the area's look in the 15th and 16th Centuries. A sign for a long-gone pharmacy is still visible.

In the late 1800's, chemist Charles Delacre was an owner of pharmacies in Brussels. At the time, chocolate was, above all, used as a medical cure. Delacre eventually became so well known for his chocolates that in 1879 he was appointed as a purveyor of the Belgian Royal house. In 1891, Delacre began to sell "Pacha Delacre" his most famous creation, a biscuit with pure Belgian chocolate.

Today, Delacre sells chocolate biscuits internationally but has only one shop in Brussels, on a small square on Vieille Halle aux Bles between Grand Place and the Sablon.

To see remnants of the last surviving Brussels mansion from the 15th Century, look to the left of the former pharmacy. The shorter buildings with the stepped roof lines are the Hotel Ravenstein. The buildings were not hotels as we know the term but stables. Today, they house scientific associations.

Point 8: Whirling Ear

The tall sculpture sitting in a small pond is one of the few surviving works from the World Exhibition of Brussels 1958. Crafted by Alexander Calder, it stood in the middle of a basin with fountains in front of the US pavilion. After the exhibition, it was dismantled and stored in a depot of the Royal Museums where it lay rusting for years before it found a new home here.

Often you will a find a bright yellow Gaufres Chaudes or Warm Waffle truck parked here. They are staples in Brussels' tourist areas.

In Belgium, a waffle is not for breakfast but an afternoon snack, traditionally served with powdered sugar but also available with ice cream or sauces. Belgians will debate which is the better waffle, the type found in Brussels or the Liege waffle. So what is the difference? The waffles served from the Brussels yellow trucks are made with thin, yeast-leavened batter which makes them lighter. They have defined edges with deeper holes. Their counterpart named after Liege, a city to the east of Brussels, is made from batter that is thicker, stickier and has chunks of sugar, which makes the waffle sweeter, crispier and gives it a golden coating. Because the dough is pushed into the waffle maker, the Liege waffle emerges with uneven edges.

Point 9: Jardin du Mont des Arts

Walk to the top of the stairs that overlook a garden. The spire of the Town Hall in Grand Place serves as the backdrop. You are standing at Mont des Arts or Hill of the Arts. The story of its construction is one of conflicting visions.

In the late 19th Century King Leopold II wanted to create an arts center on the hill overlooking the Lower Town to surround his palace with grand buildings. His goal was to project Belgium as a cultural capital of Europe. The mayor of Brussels on the other hand wanted to preserve the area's Medieval character and not disturb its thriving businesses in the Upper Town.

Leopold acted first, buying the neighborhood here in 1897 and ordering the destruction of much of the housing and the alleyways between the Place Royale and Grand Place. But in the absence of approved plans to rebuild and a lack of funding, the area lay in ruins for several years enabling the mayor to commission construction of the Flemish Revival Delacre and the Art Nouveau Old England buildings.

It was not until 1908 that King Leopold II's plans for Mont des Arts, with its panoramic view of the Lower Town, were finally revealed. It was a part of his preparation for the Universal Exposition that Brussels was to host in 1910. The plans were considered so lavish, the Belgian Parliament did not approve its funding. The project was put on hold and again the area was in development limbo.

To conceal the remaining abandoned construction sites left from the stalled vision, Leopold ordered that a temporary garden be constructed on the hill. The new Jardin du Mont des Arts featured a multi-tiered staircase with gardens and cascading fountains, creating a seamless connection between the Upper and Lower Towns. Rows of shops were built on each side, making the garden one of the Brussels most popular gathering spots.

In 1955, the "temporary" garden was demolished with a single level park taking its place. Geometric buildings, like the Royal Library and a subterranean congress hall, were constructed around the space. In the early 21st Century, the area was renovated yet again with the glass building "The Square" appearing.

Point 10: Bozar

To see how the King's vision for Mont des Arts played out, walk back to Montagne de la Cour (the street's name has changed to Coudenberg), following it down the hill as it bends to the right. Cross the street, Monts des Arts.

The modern building to your right is the Palace of Fine Arts or Bozar. Built after Leopold II's death, it is an Art Deco design based on plans by Victor Horta. When the plans were approved in 1922, three restrictions were included: The building had to be erected on a small, irregular lot; the ground floor must accommodate shops; and most importantly the height must not block the king's view of Grand Place from the Royal Palace.

Point 11: Galerie Ravenstein

Continue walking to the entrance of Galerie Ravenstein on your side of the street across from the far end of the Bozar. Go down the steps into the gallery. Under a huge dome is a long shopping corridor with glass bricks and tile covered floors. At the end near the Bozar is a mosaic covered fountain. At the main entrance at the opposite end of the gallery near Central Station are ceiling paintings depicting the winds and constellations.

Built between 1954 and 1958 as part of the city's preparations for Expo '58, the gallery is a classic example of mid-20th Century commercial urban architecture. Today it has a feel of being cut off from time and its entire surroundings, a commercial space linking the Central Station with the Bozar imagined to be bustling but holding promise never fulfilled.

Return to Point 6: Café at Musee des Instruments

Retrace your steps to exit the gallery from where you entered and cross the street to be on the same side as the Bozar. Turn right, walking up the hill to the Musical Instrument Museum in the Old England store for the debrief.

You can visit the museum if you are a fan of musical instruments or you can simply tell the guard you want to visit the cafe on the top floor. The cafe is a Debriefing Point not because of its beer list but for its sweeping views of the city. Look at the detail of the interior as the elevator ascends to the roof. You can likely imagine merchants operating out of small shops within the structure. When you reach the café, try one of the Trappist ales, perhaps a Chimay.

The Trappist order comes from La Trappe, France, where in the 17th Century a Cistercian monastery reacted to adoption of liberal practices. They emphasized tradition, including that monasteries be self-supporting. A proven solution was brewing, also a way for monasteries to feed local communities.

In 1997, eight Trappist abbeys, six from Belgium including Chimay, founded the International Trappist Association (ITA), creating a logo to prevent commercial companies from abusing the Trappist name. To earn the ITA logo, a beer must be brewed within the walls of the monastery and the revenue from sales must be used only to cover expenses with the rest used for charitable purposes.

All the Trappist brewers lay claim to their own strain of yeasts. Chimay uses a yeast that Brother Theodore isolated in 1948. The abbey produces four types of beer. Chimay Gold is flavored with muscat grapes and is 4.8% ABV. Chimay Red or Premiere has a touch of bitterness and is closest to the original Chimay Abbey beer. Chimay Triple, a triple ale, is known for its flavor of hops and yeast. Chimay Blue or Grand Reserve Chimay is the most complex and powerful of the family. A blend of Chimay beers, it is 9% ABV. Chimay also produces a range of cheeses.

Return: Walk back down Coudenberg and cross over to rue Monts des Arts to return to Central Station and the Metro. You can also walk through Galerie Ravenstein.

Walk 3
Sablon

Royal Treasures and Horse Trading

Length of Walk: 1 hour without museums or debriefs
Museum Options: Magritte Museum • Royal Museum of Fine Arts

Connecting Dots: King Leopold II envisioned situating institutions around Place Royale to make it a center of the arts. The Palais des Beaux-Arts, now one of four museums connected with the Royal Museums of Fine Arts, was completed in 1887 to house the country's most prized paintings. Centuries before, in the 16th Century, one of the Low Countries' noble families built a palace south of Coudenberg Castle, near what had been the edge of the city's southern fortifications. The area, named Sablon for the sandy hill in the area, had a long history for trade. In the Middle Ages, traders entering the city from the southeast watered their horses here before passing through the city walls to trade in the markets surrounding Grand Place. Later, the Sablon became known for horse trading, a reputation it held through the 18th Century. In the intervening years, royal residences, government offices and businesses were constructed around the Sablon, stretching to and from the Royal Palace, making the Sablon and the avenue that connected them the most desirable area of Brussels.

Starting Point: Central Station. Leave the Metro at Central Station to rue des Colonies (Cantersteen) bordering the eastern side of the station. At the southeast corner of the station, turn left crossing rue des Colonies walking uphill onto Mont des Arts. A garden will be on your right. When the street ends at Coudenberg, turn right, walking around the curve and uphill. The Magritte Museum will be on the southeast corner of Place Royale.

Walk 3 Map 1

Point 1: Magritte Museum

The Magritte Museum, a part of the Royal Museums of Belgium, displays more than 200 of artist Rene Magritte's works, including oils on canvas, gouaches, drawings, sculptures and painted objects as well as advertising posters, musical scores, vintage photographs and films.

Magritte was born in 1898 in Hainaut, Belgium. He began his art career as a wallpaper designer and commercial artist. His early paintings were executed under the influence of Cubism and Futurism. Later, while living in Paris, he adopted the style of the Surrealists, establishing close friendships with Max Ernst, Salvador Dali and Joan Miro.

In Paris, Magritte's system of conceptual painting was formed. It remained almost unchanged until the end of his life. Demonstrating the confusion of visual perception and illusionary of images, Magritte used the symbols of mirrors, eyes, windows, stages, curtains and pictures within pictures to depict trustworthy an unreal, unthinkable reality.

As someone who preferred to stay at home, Magritte painted everyday objects. "Is this a pipe? No it is a painting" sums up his most famous work. It revealed the basis of his intellect, the pitting of assumption against truth. Known for sleeping 12 hours a day, Magritte was asked if he slept to dream. To sleep, he replied.

Magritte died in 1967.

Point 2: Royal Museums of Fine Arts of Belgium

Head next store to visit two of the other Royal Museums of Fine Arts: The Museum of Ancient Art and the Museum of Modern Art.

The building itself was commissioned by King Leopold and completed in 1897 as one of the King's projects aimed at making Brussels the artistic capital of Europe. It is an example of the Beaux-Arts architecture style taught in Paris in the 18th and 19th Centuries. The style is notable for the use of statuary and over-scaled details which reveal the purpose of the building. Belgian Alphonse Balat was Leopold II's principal architect, making the Beaux-Arts style the distinctive architectural statement of government buildings during Brussels' late 19th Century transformation.

The collections housed in the two museums contain over 20,000 works from the 15th Century to the present. Notable are its collection of paintings by Bruegel and other Flemish artists. The Rubens Room houses more than 20 paintings by the artist.

After leaving the museums turn right and walk along rue de la Régence toward the Palace of Justice, the huge building with the gold dome.

Point 3: Garden of Sculptures

Adjacent to the buildings of the Museums of Fine Arts, an outdoor garden features the museum's collection of sculptures. Most depict the female figure. The garden was opened in 1992 on the site of Brussels first botanical garden. There is no cost to enter.

Continue towards the gold dome along rue de la Regence.

Walk 3 Map 2

Point 4: Church of Our Lady of Sablon

You are in the Sablon. Beginning from the 16th Century, the residential area around the palace of Brussels extended further and further southward along what is now rue de la Regence. The Church of Our Lady of Sablon will be on the right.

In the first centuries of Brussels' existence, the Sablon was a sandy hill situated south of the First Wall, adjacent to open wetlands and grasslands. A hermit is said to have made the area his home. The French word "sablon" and Dutch "zavel" mean a fine-grained sand, halfway between silt and sand.

In the 13th Century, the area came into the possession of the Saint-Jean Hospital located to the southeast. The hospital needed additional burial space when their own cemetery had become full, perhaps a statement about the medical staff's healing capabilities.

In 1304, the hospital sold the land to the crossbowmen's guild. In 1318, they completed construction of a chapel on the site, spurring the creation of a small settlement.

Legend has it that in 1348 the Virgin Mary spoke to a woman in Antwerp, instructing her to assist the people of Brussels who were in the grips of the Black Death. The woman secured, or rather stole, what was said to be a miracle-working statue of the Virgin Mary, taking it by boat down the River Senne from Antwerp to Brussels. As she was instructed in her vision, she presented it to the crossbow-men for their chapel in the Sablon. The statue of Mary was solemnly placed in the chapel, drawing pilgrims to the once isolated area.

As a tribute to the gift, the crossbowmen embarked on a campaign to expand their church following Gothic traditions, promising to hold an annual procession in which the statue was carried through Brussels. The procession is the Ommegang, a word for "walking around" in Old Flemish. Beginning in the 15th Century the event took on a material meaning, displaying wealth, power and glamour associated with the royal families that ruled the Belgian lands over the years. The event still takes place.

Among the church's most striking features are its stained glass windows. As was common in the Middle Ages, houses originally surrounded the church, but they, like much of Brussels, fell victim to one of King Leopold II's urbanization projects in the late 19th Century.

Point 5: Petit Sablon

Across rue de La Regence is the Petit Sablon, a neo-Rennaissance style garden opened in 1890. A wrought iron railing divided by 48 columns encloses the space. A bronze statue representing the city's traditional crafts and trades caps each column. Four statues are crowned: the masons, the stone-cutters, the sculptors and the slate-quarry workers, illustrating their special status. Within the garden, the nine beds of trimmed boxwood represent the nine Belgian provinces of the era. Another bed in the shape of a crown symbolizes Belgium. The garden occupies the land that was the cemetery of the Saint-Jean Hospital.

In the center of the garden, a statue pair depicts Counts Egmont and Hornes, noblemen who were decapitated by the city's Spanish rulers in 1568 for their criticism of the Spanish inquisition. Their execution helped to spark the uprising which led to the region's independence from Spain. The monument was originally in Grand Place in front of the Maison du Roi, the site of their execution, and a poke to the eye of Spanish king. It was moved to the Sablon in 1879.

Marble statues of ten distinguished Belgians of the 16th Century sit in a semicircle around Egmont and Hornes. The small shed is the work place of the groundskeeper.

Egmont's Palace up the hill on the eastern side of the Petit Sablon was built between 1548 and 1560 in the Flemish gothic style. In subsequent years, it was modified for Renaissance tastes and later altered to reflect the Classical style it has today.

Point 6: Grand Sablon

Exit the garden to enter the Grand Sablon, heading back to rue de la Regence, walking down the hill with the Church of our Lady of Sablon on your right to enter the Grand Sablon. Stop at the fountain in the middle of the square behind the church.

With its location just outside the city's fortifications, the Sablon was a resting place for merchants travelling to Grand Place. From the 15th Century it became a market area largely known for the horse trading that took place every Friday until the mid-18th Century. The Fountain of Minerva in the center of the square is where an artificial water reservoir served as a drinking trough for animals and as a water reserve in case of fire. The reservoir was replaced by a fountain in 1661, which in turn was replaced with the current fountain in 1751. Straw was stored on what is today rue de la Paille at the bottom of the square to the right of the roundabout.

In the 17th and 18th Centuries, the Grand Sablon was the wealthiest section of Brussels, home to aristocratic families who built townhomes within a short carriage ride of the Royal Palace. They still stand, though no longer residences, around the square.

In the 19th Century, the Sablon would lose its "wealthiest distinction" to the Leopold Quarter as the city's development turned eastward.

Meanwhile working class families populated the neighboring area southwest to be near the small factories that operated further down the hill.

Today the town homes that surround the square are filled with upscale commercial enterprises, notably chocolate. Pierre Marcolini's is among the most famous. The open-air market experience continues, but instead of horses being traded, antiques are sold on weekends from awning-covered stalls.

Point 7: Ruins of the First Wall

Continue down the hill away from the church, walking along the sidewalk on the left side of the square. Follow the sidewalk to the left of the roundabout crossing rue des Minimes and rue Joseph Stephens until you find the walking street, rue de Rollebeek on your left on the western side of the square. It is an ancient passage that feeds into the Lower Town from the Grand Sablon.

Walk down Rollebeek past a collection of restaurants and shops turning right when it ends. A gas station and bowling alley await you. For a view of the city, you can go inside and visit the bowling alley's top floor. Otherwise, walk a few steps further to find a section of the First Wall that surrounded Brussels.

Clay was used when construction began at the end of the 11th Century to create a circle of walls 7 meters (23 feet) high and 2.3 meters (7.5 feet) thick. They were linked by a series of arches for support. A wooden fence sat on top for further protection, and a large ditch in front could be flooded to create a moat. The clay was later replaced with sandstone, extending the height to 10 meters (32 feet). Travelers could enter the city through seven main gateways. Visitors from the south entered through a gate near here.

What remains here are the ruins of one of the 50 original fortification towers. It is easy to imagine soldiers perched on top, watching the countryside for aggressors, and shooting arrows through the slits if they approached.

Reverse your steps to where Rollebeek ended. Turn right onto rue des Alexiens, turning your back to Rollebeek and the Sablon and crossing Boulevard de l'Empereur.

Point 8: La Porte Noire

Across the street from a small park, 67 rue des Alexiens is dark and foreboding at the entrance. Once you step down into the cellar you will find La Porte Noire, the perfect place for a dark Belgian beer. Be forewarned, this former kitchen for a 17th Century convent does not normally open until 5:00 PM and usually not at all on Sundays. There are many choices here, among them Val-Dieu Grand Cru, an abbey strong ale beer. A frequent draft option is Brusseleir, a dark IPA distinguished by its rich malt character and light chocolate notes from the local Brasserie de la Senne

Point 9: La Fleur en Papier Dore

If it is time for lunch or dinner, 55 rue des Alexiens hosts a small restaurant that was a haunt of Magritte and other surrealists. It is the perfect place for a debrief where you can enjoy typical Brussels fare. If you would like a thirst quencher, try Lindemans Gueuze Cuvée René.

Return: Walk back to the bowling alley near the ruins of the First Wall, turning left on Boulevard de l'Empereur. A short distance away is Central Station and the Metro. Otherwise you can continue to walk away from the Sablon along rue des Alexiens to the Anneessens underground tram station where you can connect to the Metro.

Walk 4
Cinquantenaire Parc

Building a European Capital

Length of Walk: 1.5 hours without museum options or debriefs

Museum Options: Royal Museum of Art and History • AutoWorld • Royal Museum of Armed Forces & Military History • Temple of Human Passions

Connecting Dots: To serve as the home of a national exhibition commemorating the 50th anniversary of the Belgian State's founding, King Leopold II opened Cinquantenaire Parc in 1880. The park's design epitomized his vision for Brussels to be among the top tier of European capitals. Its creation provided him with a venue to showcase the country's innovation and industry. Buildings styled after London's Kensington Palace formed bookends for a triumphal arch lying at the park's heart. Leading to the east from the park's center, Avenue de Tervueren, created for the 1897 World's Fair held at the park, opened a path to expanding suburbs and an outlying pavilion housing treasures taken from the king's African colony. Exquisite town homes and apartments lined each side of the grand avenue, many the works of prominent architects. The scene of the park with a grand arch in its center provided a spectacular vista to those entering Brussels via carriage, street car or automobile. An entire new section of Brussels had been created. Now is forms the backdrop for the European Union District.

Starting Point: Entrance to Metro at Merode on Avenue Tervueren.

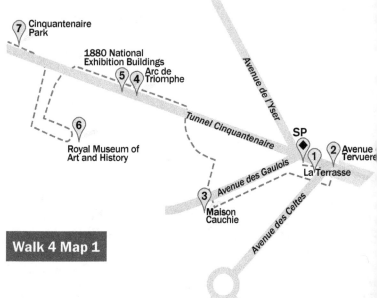

Walk 4 Map 1

Point 1: La Terrasse

Consider visiting La Terrasse on the south side of Avenue Tervueren at the Metro entrance before you begin your walk. The arch with Art Nouveau lettering makes it unmistakable. Specialties here are the Maredsous abbey beers: Blond at 6%, Brune Dubbel at 8%, and the Trippel at 10%.

Point 2: Avenue de Tervueren

After your beer, step outside and turn your back to the park, looking down Avenue de Tervueren, an elegant boulevard built by King Leopold II for the Brussels International Exposition held in 1897. Today, it leads to Brussels' early 20th Century suburbs. Some of the town homes that align it have been converted into foreign embassies or office buildings.

The 1897 Brussels International Exhibition, with the automobile as its symbol, opened on May 10 and closed on November 8. Twenty-seven countries participated, and nearly 8 million people visited. After the 1897 exhibition, Brussels hosted three other International or World Exhibitions: In 1910 with Industries as the theme; 1935 highlighting Colonization; and 1958 heralding a More Human World.

Cinquantenaire Park was the scene of the 1897 and 1910 International Exhibitions and the 1880 Belgium National Exhibition.

Avenue de Tervueren was an important component of the 1897 exhibition's design. It connected the Cinquantenaire Park, the fair's focal point, with an exhibit at the Royal Estate in Tervueren. There, artifacts of King Leopold II's personal property, the Congo Free State, were displayed in a specially built Palace of the Colonies. Belgium, or more precisely the king, only had one colony but the king did not lack for vision nor bravado. A tramway, now Line 44, was included in the construction of Avenue de Tervueren to link the two sites.

King Leopold's personal ownership of the Congo Free State was recognized by the Berlin Conference of 1884-85. Belgium's Parliament had little interest in supporting colonization so the King borrowed the money, from Parliament, to own it himself.

Hosting an international exhibition enabled the King to show off Belgium's industrial, artistic, and commercial prowess and to attract investors for both Belgium and the king's African country.

Formal gardens designed by the French landscape architect Elie Lainé surrounded the Palace of the Colonies. In the main hall was a distinctive Art Nouveau structure built of wood from African trees meant to evoke the African forest. The exhibit featured the Congo's export products, coffee, cacao and tobacco. The most popular attraction was an African village, built on the grounds outside the pavilion, in which 60 Africans lived.

Point 3: Maison Cauchie

If you would like an Art Nouveau detour, walk down Avenue des Gaulois, the street along the left side of the park away from the roundabout. The first street on the left is rue des Francs. At No. 5 is Maison Cauchie, the former house of artists Paul and Caroline Cauchie. It is open to the public every first weekend of the month. The façade of the building is frequently shown in Brussels tour books. "Par nous, pour nous," or "By us, for us," is written on one of the Cauchies' murals.

Cross Avenue des Gaulois entering the park walking to the pond. Stop in front of the arch.

Point 4: Arc de Triomphe – And Walk to the Top

One element in Leopold II's plan to enhance the stature of the Belgian capital was the creation of Parc du Cinquantenaire. Formerly the exercise grounds of the Belgian Army, the park was built to host the 1880 National Exhibition commemorating the 50th anniversary of Belgian independence. Its pentagon shape represents the city's outline as formed by the Second Medieval Wall.

The centerpiece is the triumphal arch. It took more than 25 years to complete due to tension between the king, who commissioned the arch, and the Belgian Parliament who had to pay for it. Because only the bases of the columns were in place when the fair opened in 1880, the rest of the arch was built with wooden panels. These wooden panels stayed in place for the 1897 Brussels International Exposition and for other exhibitions and festivals until 1905 when the arch as seen today was completed, just in time to mark the 75th anniversary of the Belgian state's founding.

On top of the arch sits a bronze quadriga, or chariot, guided by a woman representing Brabant raising the national flag. Allegoric statues at the foot of the columns represent the other eight provinces of Belgium. On the sides of the columns, mosaics added between 1920 and 1932 glorify the "peace loving nation of Belgium," a statement reflecting on the destruction in the country caused by World War I.

Inside the building which houses the Royal Museum of the Armed Forces and Military History visitors can climb to the top of the arch for a panoramic view of the city. As soon as you enter, go to the left. Follow the signs for "Panorama." A doorway around the corner leads to stairs (and an elevator) reaching to the top of the arch. You do not have pay the museum's entry fee to visit the top.

Point 5: 1880 National Exhibition Buildings

The buildings surrounding the arch date from the 1880 National Exhibition.

The north building remains as it was originally designed by architect Gideon Bordiau. This is the building to your right if Avenue de Turvueren at your back. It and its sister building on the southern side of the park were designed in the same style as Kensington

Palace in London. The symmetry of the design was destroyed when the southern building was rebuilt after a fire in the 1950s.

The north building houses the Royal Military Museum, interesting for those with a military passion. The museum's collection includes equipment abandoned by the Germans when they left Belgium at the end of World War I. One way the Belgians responded to the German invasion of World War I was to ban the sale of German beer in Brussels cafes.

The south building is home to AutoWorld Museum for car lovers and those interested in European motoring. The south building also houses the Royal Museum of Art and History.

Point 6: Royal Museum of Art and History

Enter the Royal Museum of Art and History by walking under the arch, and turning left. Continue around the entire side of the building. The museum's entrance is set back after you turn the corner.

The museum's collection dates from the 15th to 17th Centuries when it began with diplomatic gifts, mementoes and curiosa owned by Burgundian dukes and subsequently the Habsburg archdukes. In 1906 the non-military items were moved to the building here. A fire in 1946 that reduced an entire wing of the museum to ashes destroyed some of the collection, but it was rapidly rebuilt in the renovated wing.

The museum traces the history of the land that is today Belgium and boasts an impressive collection of European decorative arts from the Middle Ages to the 20th Century. Through its tapestry displays, the power of Brussels as a Medieval trading center comes alive.

Brussels was on the trade route between Bruges and Ghent and Cologne. At the height of its economic prominence, Brussels exported luxury items such as fabrics and tapestries to Paris and Venice. In the 15th Century, half the population of Brussels earned its livelihood from tapestries.

Within the museum is The Plaster-cast Workshop, established in the 19th Century. It boasts a collection of more than 4,000 casts dating from prehistoric times. In reproducing their works of art, craftsmen employ traditional techniques in both the casting and the patination. The workshop sells plaster casts as souvenirs.

After exiting the museum, head to the center of the park and walk down the esplanade to the opposite end of the park from where you entered.

Point 7: Cinquantenaire Park

If you happen to have a bottle of wine or Trappist beer in your pack, take a while to sit and watch residents enjoy the open space.

Sitting in Cinquantenaire today, it is difficult to imagine that from the 1880s to 1920s, pavilions, food stands, and amusement rides lined today's peaceful strolling paths.

Similarly, the visitors to the park then could not imagine that one day a roadway would pass under their feet, part of the massive construction that transformed Brussels for the 1958 World's Fair and extended the city to far suburbs.

Industrial exhibitions were always important to Belgium. Leopold II used them to showcase the little country's European prominence as an industrial power and intellectual center. The country hosted major national and international events on a roughly 25-year cycle beginning in 1855 to commemorate major anniversaries of its founding as an independent state.

As Cinquantenaire Park became too small for exhibitions planned after the dawn of the 20th Century, the city chose a new exhibition area north of Brussels' center in the Heysel plains, a field that had been prepared for urbanization during the reign of Leopold II but was never developed.

To highlight its recovery from World War I, Belgium's bid to host the World Exhibition of 1935 was selected. More than 180 buildings were constructed at Heysel, including the main hall, an Art Deco centerpiece. More than 300 congresses, parades, festivals and concerts were organized. Attendance exceeded 20 million. To celebrate the 50th anniversary of the founding of the Congo Free State and the fair's theme of Colonization, Belgium created a human zoo as part of a Congolese village. The ample grounds at Heysel also accommodated a giant amusement park and a reconstruction of "old Brussels."

With the Belgian cycle calling for another fair after World War II, the country was awarded the World's Fair of 1958. Expo 58, as it was called, took place at Heysel with many of the buildings from the 1935 fair reused. A notable addition was the Atomium, a stainless-steel model of an elementary iron crystal, magnified 165 billion times. Forty-one million visitors attended the fair, whose theme called for a "More Human World" based on world peace and social and economic progress.

Continue to walk away from the arch to the northwest corner of the park. There you will find a square building fronted by four columns.

Point 8: Temple of Human Passions

The Temple of Human Passions was designed by Victor Horta for the 1897 fair to house a sculpture by Jef Lambeaux. At first glance, the building features classic Greek temple design, but hints at the emerging Art Nouveau style of a young Horta are evident. Modifications carried out in 1909 and 1910 altered the design, but when the building was constructed it had not one straight line. For example, the walls are slightly bent at their base like how the trunk of a tree meets the ground.

Soon after its completion, the building was closed to the public. It was not even open for viewing at the 1897 fair for which it was built. A dispute between Horta and Lambeaux concerning how the sculpture should be displayed was one source of contention. Lambeaux objected to the sculpture being visible from outside the building.

There was another reason why the building was closed. The artwork inside included nudes engaging in carnal activity. That did not win public favor in the largely Roman Catholic country. The sculpture is an allegorical representation of the pleasures and sorrows of humanity. The lower level has representations of maternity, seduction and suicide. The middle level portrays debauchery, joy, rape, war and remorse. The entire composition is dominated by death. What a joyful experience to share with the family on a Sunday afternoon at a fair aimed at promoting national prosperity!

The building was opened on a more regular basis after Horta agreed to structural changes. But soon it was closed again. Beginning in 2002 the temple was open one hour per day. Today, after another renovation, the building is open on a more regular (irregular) basis.

At the time of this guide's writing, it is open on Wednesday, Saturday and Sunday from around 10 am to 4 and only between March or April and October.

Point 9: Grande Mosque

Next to the Temple of Human Passions is the Grand Mosque. The building was constructed to form the Oriental Pavilion of the National Exhibition held in 1880. The building deteriorated in the 20th Century until the 1960s when it was given to the King of Saudi Arabia who refurbished it as a center for study of Islam.

Leave the park by turning to the Grande Mosque and walking around its right side. Make a semi-circle around the mosque, exiting the park to the right of the mosque. Go left upon leaving the park on Avenue de la Renaissance. Immediately cross Avenue de Cortenberg at the crosswalk for northbound traffic and then at the crosswalk for southbound. Backtrack on Avenue de Cortenberg to take the first street to the left, Avenue Michel Ange. Admire the Flemish style and Art Nouveau buildings before the street ends at a square.

Point 10: The Squares

Cross the street. You are in Square Ambiorix, the middle of three squares. To your right is the smaller Square Marguerite and to the left or west is Square Marie Louise. They are all the work of Gedeon Bordiau, the same architect who designed the buildings surrounding the Arc de Triomphe. His design for Cinquantenaire Park and the residential squares were part of King Leopold II's grand design to connect city of Brussels with its growing suburbs and an early attempt at urban planning.

A cascading garden was designed to use water draining downhill from Marguerite to Marie Louise to create a large pond for water fowl. For years, the city would collect the ducks and geese before the ponds were about to freeze.

Walk to the right following the perimeter of Square Ambiorix. The town homes along the squares show a fundamental concept of Art Nouveau, diversity with unity, classic examples of late 19th Century Belle de Epoque, a period of affluence and artistic creativity that ended with World War I.

Point 11: Maison Saint-Cyr

Stop at No. 11 Square Ambiorix, Maison Saint-Cyr. It is only 3.6 meters (11.7 feet) wide for a length of 19.5 meters (64 feet). A central staircase has a glass ceiling to allow for natural light. The town home was built for the painter Georges Saint-Cyr in 1903 by Gustave Strauven, who at age 18 began working for the father of Art Nouveau, Victor Horta.

Art Nouveau swept Brussels from the 1890s to the start of World War I. More than an architectural style, it represented a way of thinking. Its adherents used it to argue for social causes, such as the fight against oppression of women and to trumpet new construction technologies. Iron ornamentation, female figures, and natural lighting characterize the Art Nouveau town home, with a nod given to buildings as machines for living. When designing an Art Nouveau home, architects considered the preferences of occupants such as how they wished to greet guests and spend leisure time making the home highly personal.

World War 1 doomed Art Nouveau. Money was tight. Mass construction was required for the reconstruction that followed the war. The European spirit was broken.

Continue walking along Square Ambiorix. Avenue Palmerston is the short street that joins Square Ambiorix to Square Marie-Louise. Three town homes on the avenue were designed by Horta himself: Hotel Delhaye (No. 2); Hotel Deprez-Van de Velde (No. 3); and Hotel van Eetvelde at (No. 4).

Designed in 1895, No. 4 is noteworthy for its use of steel, uncommon at the time for non-industrial construction. Horta used it here to build the façade in this elegant town home built for Edmond van Eetvelde, the administrator of the Congo Free State. Light entered a central reception area from a stained-glass cupola, making use of glass in a way also uncommon for residential construction. The building at No. 2 Avenue Palmerston with the detailed sandstone façade is an extension designed by Horta in 1898 to house a garage and office for van Eetvelde as well as apartments.

At the pond, turn left, cutting across the divider in Avenue Palmerston. Walk back up to Square Ambiorix, this time staying on the side with the square to your left. Rue Archimede exits the square at its middle. Walk down rue Archimede towards the EU complex. When you pass rue Stevin, the next point is on your right.

Point 12: Berlaymont Building

The European Commission arrived in Brussels in 1958. By 1965, the commission had more than 3,200 staff scattered across eight buildings. The Belgian government, hoping to consolidate its position as host of the commission, offered to build an administrative complex to accommodate all the commission's staff.

The land they chose was the 300-year-old home of a girls' school, Dames du Berlaymont, in the Leopold Quarter. The building that rose on the site was named after the school and was an architectural marvel when it opened in 1967. The cruciform design reminiscent of early Christian churches has four wings of unequal lengths resting on columns which along with the glass facade create the illusion that the building is floating in air. The architect's vision was for the building to defy the harness of history and aspire man to new ideals.

Throughout the 1970s and 80s the Belgian government further invested in the construction of EU buildings in the area, making the remaining residents fear the area was becoming a bureaucratic ghetto. With the government arguing that the chaotic speculation that characterized the transition of the Leopold Quarter from a residential area to a commercial one decades before had a far worse impact than the transformation of the area into a "European Quarter," residents could do little to stem the tide of redevelopment. Architectural competitions were held to at least add diversity to the building landscape rather than repeating the monotony of the area's mid-20th Century office construction.

Today about 10% of the city is said to have a connection to the international community, and 62% of the city's population was born abroad or are from recent migrant backgrounds. (In 1842, 7.5% of Brussels' 113,207 inhabitants were foreign citizens, mostly from neighboring countries.) The EU consumes half of Brussels' 3.5 million square meters (38 million square feet) of occupied office space. Not only does the EU pay an estimated 1 billion Euros to the city annually for fees and services, Brussels restaurants and hotels benefit from the diplomats, journalists and tourists who visit.

Walk back along Archimedes in the direction of the squares stopping at the main intersection before them.

Point 13: La Fontaine or Le Coin Du Diable

La Fontaine, Archimedes Street 6/8, is a wine bar but still a relaxing place to debrief. It is surrounded by Irish pubs at the intersection of rue Stevin if you would prefer a good Irish stout. If your choice is La Fontaine, try a Lindemans Krieg, a lambic beer that is infused with cherries. It looks like a sparkling wine so why not try it at a wine bar. To make krieg, sour Morello cherries are fermented with the lambic.

For local flavor, Le Coin Du Diable, or the Devil's Corner, is across the intersection. Several beers are on draft, usually including Maredsous. The abbey beer dates from the 1870s, but unlike its Trappist cousins, monks are not involved in the brewing. Still the centuries old recipe is used, following Benedictine traditions.

Return: After you debrief, find the entrance to the Metro on the eastern and western sides of the Berlaymont Building on rue de la Loi.

Walk 5
Leopold Quarter

The EU Comes to Brussels

Length of Walk: 1.5 hours without museum options or debriefs

Museum Options: Parliamentarium • Wiertz Museum • House of European History

Connecting Dots: The royals of the Brabant court used the eastern lands outside the city walls for hunting and picnicking. Later, merchants and others seeking the patronage of the court built homes here, making the area one of Brussels first suburbs. It was named the Leopold Quarter after Belgium's first two kings. With streets laid out in a grid pattern to allow for squares and with nearby amenities like a zoo and English style garden, the Leopold Quarter became the most prestigious section of Brussels by mid-19th Century. After World War II, the area fell victim to "Brusselsization," a term coined to describe haphazard urban development. The grid pattern that created carefully planned squares now lent itself to the interests of developers who constructed nondescript office buildings. City officials converted graceful boulevards to motorways. With the Leopold Quarter in transition, Belgium politicians saw an opportunity to use the land as a lure to attract the European Union beginning another phase of massive urban development.

Starting Point: Entrance to the Metro at Trone on rue du Luxembourg, the street that ends to the east with a glass building towering over it.

Walk 5 Map 1

Point 1: The Small Ring Road

The Metro entrance at Trone is also the first vantage point on the walk.

Stand at the intersection with rue du Luxembourg turning your attention to Boulevard du Regent. Look south, in the direction of roadway that is straight and slightly uphill.

Boulevard du Regent is one of the roads that creates the Inner or Small Ring surrounding Brussels city center. If you look at a map of Brussels, the Small Ring is the pentagon shape that encloses the city.

The ring traces the path of the Second Wall that encircled Brussels. The need for the Second Wall became apparent by the attack of Flemish forces in the 14th Century when artillery fire reached the center of Brussels from the boundaries of the First Wall.

If you were standing here between the 15th to 18th Centuries, you would be just outside a brick and stone wall eight meters (25 feet) high. Built from 1356 to 1383, it included 72 semicircular and seven main gates. The gates corresponded to the entry points located in the city's First Wall built at the end of the 11th Century. That wall was located about 270 meters (300 yards) to your right, inside the park and adjacent to today's Royal Palace. In other sections of the city the distance between the walls was far greater.

The gate to enter the city from the east was located at Porte de Namur, today one Metro stop to the south. When night fell, a bell rang and the Second Wall's seven gates closed. Soldiers stood guard on top. Outside the wall were forest and meandering streams. Inside was Coudenberg Palace and homes owned by patrons of the Brabant Court.

Strengthened in the 16th and 17th Centuries, the Second Wall fell into disrepair in the 18th Century. In 1810 Napoleon Bonaparte issued a decree to demolish what remained and construct boulevards in its place.

Now imagine it is 1890. Standing at the same point looking in the same direction, you would see a pedestrian path bordered on each side by a roadway for carriages. On the right and left, small shops sold premium goods. Brussels was at the peak of its prosperity, the capital of one of the richest nations on Earth.

Napoleon's decree to construct boulevards was seized upon by King Leopold II a few decades later to transform the city into a major European capital. A statue of Leopold II on horseback can be seen at the entrance to the Royal Park to your right across the boulevard.

No section of the Small Ring epitomized that plan more than the stretch lying before you. Like today, it connected the Royal Palace with the picturesque Avenue Louise about a quarter mile to the south. The expanse of its width was meant to impress visiting royalty and businessmen, and the walking path bisecting the two roadways offered tranquility in the midst of commerce and transportation.

Behind you to the north and around the bend are several foreign embassies, including those of the US, France and Russia. For a quick exercise in world politics, compare their security. They are on the left (western) side of the boulevard as you look north.

Standing next to Boulevard du Regent, you can see the impact of a fundamental fact of Brussels' evolution. Cars whiz by on either side.

Because green space was easily accessible near to the city and its residents had the wealth to build single family homes, Brussels has been a city of commuters from as early as the 19th Century.

Fueled by development after the destruction of World War II, preparations for the 1958 World's Fair, and a Belgian love affair with everything American, Brussels embraced the automobile. The grand boulevards and pedestrian walkways were gutted for vehicular tunnels and additional lanes for traffic. City officials in the early 1950s imagined they were building a model European city of the future. Instead they destroyed much of Brussels' past. Photographs of the roadways taken when they first opened show an occasional automobile, a much different scene from the traffic clogged arteries they are today.

Head east along rue du Luxembourg toward the glass building.

Point 2: Square de Meeus

You are walking through the Leopold Quarter. After two blocks, Square de Meeus is on either side of rue du Luxembourg. The square and others like it were created by the grid pattern of the streets forming urban oases for residents of surrounding town mansions. The pattern dates from when the area was established after the 1830 Belgian revolution. In the late 19th and early 20th Centuries, the Leopold Quarter was Brussels most prestigious residential section.

In the 1960s, the design had an unintended consequence. The grid pattern made it easy for speculators to build office buildings, rectangular blocks of concrete and steel to which workers came in the morning and left in the evening. One after another, town mansions were torn down. As the city lured the burgeoning European Union bureaucracy in the 1970s and 80s, the transformation accelerated making much of the area an office ghetto.

The square is named after Ferdinand de Meeus, a financier who helped create the Leopold Quarter in 1838. It hosts three sculptures and four busts and has several trees each a century old. The most striking sculpture is entitled "Winged Spirit," the golden angel with arms extended upwards grieving the death of the sculptor who created it, Julien Dillens. His likeness is carved into the base. Inaugurated in 1909, it is said to be Brussels' most touched statue.

Rubbing the angel's right arm is rumored to bring good luck in love for a year. Another oddity is that the artist created the monument in his own honor.

Situated around the square, a few town mansions remain such as Numbers 19 and 20 on the southeastern corner.

Continue walking along rue du Luxembourg to the east until it ends at the square in front of the glass building.

Point 3: Place du Luxembourg

The building directly behind the square is the Brussels-Luxembourg train station, originally named Gare du Quarter Leopold. After the station opened in 1854, plans were commissioned to add a large public square in front of it. Built in the Neoclassical style to be as symmetrical as possible, the square immediately filled with shops and cafes.

In 1989, the landscape changed dramatically. The tracks of the open-air train station were covered, and in 2004 the bulk of the train station was destroyed. The platforms and ticket counters were moved underground with only the former central entrance left standing.

In the center of the square is a statue of John Cockerill. An early 19th Century industrialist known as the founder of Belgian manufacturing, Cockerill expanded the family's British-based business in the wool industry to include steam engines for ships, steam locomotives and factories for producing cloth, linen and paper. The motto "Work and Intelligence" is engraved on the statue.

Walk around the square to the train station and cross rue de Treves. Go through the passageway to the left of the rail station. You are standing on the Esplanade of the European Parliament at the doorstep of the European Union.

Point 4: European Parliament

You have passed many buildings with connections to the European Union on your walk along rue du Luxembourg. Now you are entering the complex that comprises the European Parliament. The dome of the Paul-Henri Spaak building that you saw from rue du Luxembourg mirrors the train station's clock. Spaak was a Belgian politician active in the founding of the EU.

EU institutions are spread among four European cities: Brussels, Frankfurt, Strasbourg and Luxembourg. It is Brussels, however, that has come to be known as the European capital because all the EU's institutions report to offices in Brussels and Brussels hosts the European Council, the body composed of the heads of state of each member country. Brussels is also home of the EU's Commission, the secretariat of the EU Parliament, and the Economic and Social Committee.

Throughout the 1970s and 80s the Belgian government further invested in the construction of EU buildings in the area despite objections of locals who saw their once elegant neighborhood become a bureaucratic ghetto. The government argued that the chaotic speculation that characterized the transition of the Leopold Quarter from a residential area to a commercial one decades before had a far worse impact than the transformation of the area into a "European Quarter."

There was no stopping the transformation. To avoid reinforcing the building monotony from decades before, architectural competitions added diversity to the landscape. Still, longtime residents lament the demolition of local bars and restaurants, complaining redirected and dead-ended streets have changed forever their neighborhood walks.

Today, the EU employs more than 20,000 civil servants in Brussels and occupies about fifteen percent of the city's office space.

Point 5: Parlamentarium

Turn your back to the train station and rue du Luxembourg. The building on the left with the blue sign is the EU's Parlamentarium. Inside exhibits trace the history of the EU and describe its impact on European life. Take the self-guided tour and you will leave understanding that the EU was formed as a response to the national strife, discord and destruction that engulfed Europe during the two World Wars. You will also leave thinking the European Parliament creates a lot of regulation.

Leave the Parlamentarium turning right. Go to where there is opening between the buildings on your left. Walk down the flight of stairs, heading away from Place du Luxembourg, stopping at rue Wiertz.

Cross rue Wiertz and turn right. A short distance away is a round-about. Bear to the left onto rue Vautier. Number 62 is the former house and studio of 19th Century Belgian artist Antoine Wiertz.

Point 6: Wiertz Museum

Antoine Wiertz painted religious subjects with allegorical themes in a style that attempted to combine Raphaël, Michelangelo and Rubens. Look at the foregrounds and backgrounds in Wiertz's works and you will find torsos and faces that add complexity to his paintings. Not pleased with the shiny effect of oil painting, Wiertz painted giant canvasses with a mixture of colors, turpentine and gasoline to create a mat effect. The style enabled him to work quickly as if painting a fresco. It is also the reason why his paintings are slowing eating away at the canvass.

Towards the end of his life, Wiertz persuaded the Belgian government to fund construction of a large studio next to his home. The conditions were that all of Wiertz's paintings would remain intact as a single collection and that they would continue to be displayed after his death. A final condition was that there would never be an entry fee. Unfortunately, he did not stipulate the hours of the museum's opening. It is closed on weekends and on Mondays.

Lave the museum turning left and cross rue Vautier. A few steps away will be an opening in a brick wall that leads into Leopold Park. Follow the path as it curves to the right and turn left onto a dirt walkway that leads downhill. When it ends, turn left along another path, passing by a white stone building on your right (former Institute of Sociology), the domed building (former School of Commerce). At the "T" go the right between two buildings (the former Institute of Physiology on the right and the Eastman Foundation on the left). Find a bench along the pond where you can read about the park's history and its buildings.

Point 7: Leopold Park and House of European History

A stream called the Maelbeek (millstream) ran through the center of the valley that lies between today's EU and the center city. You are in that low lying land now.

In the 15th Century, the area became popular as hunting grounds and a holiday resort for nobles living in and around Coudenberg Castle. The stream formed 58 ponds in what is today the Greater Brussels area. The pond here is one of the few that remain.

After the Medieval wall surrounding Brussels was demolished at the start of the 19th Century and Belgium gained its independence in 1830, a building frenzy followed. The area outside the eastern wall was second to none when it came to development. Town mansions lined the grid-patterned blocks. At the end of the 19th Century, the Maelbeek was diverted into sewers, and a stone bridge was built to connect the area to the Upper Town.

The park is in the former estate of Knight Dubois de Blanco, a scion of the noble Eggevoort family. In 1851 the Royal Society of Zoology purchased the estate, converting the land into what it called a "pleasure garden," complete with a zoo and English style gardens. An abandoned entrance gate and ticket stand sit at the north entrance to the park to your left. Residents could visit the pleasure gardens for a Belgian Franc on Sundays, Mondays and Thursdays and the September holidays. Shareholders' admittance was free.

Poor management and an epidemic led to the society's bankruptcy in 1876. The City of Brussels purchased the gardens in 1877. A year later, the Belgian State acquired the Redemptorists' convent next to the park transforming the convent into the Royal Belgian Institute of Natural Sciences.

In 1880, on the 50th anniversary of Belgium's independence, the park was renamed after the first two kings of the Belgians. The City of Brussels decided that Leopold Park would henceforth be opened to the general public and used for fairs.

Beginning in 1887, the park accommodated the Horticulture Internationale, a nursery housing the collections of Brussels' botanist, explorer and orchid expert Jean-Jules Linden. He introduced a variety of 650 plants to Europe. In 1908, the company, led by Linden's son, dissolved, and the greenhouses were destroyed, replaced by buildings that would be occupied by the Pasteur Institute. You walked past its remains upon entering the park.

Another late 19th Century transformation was the dedication of Leopold Park as the home of Belgium's scientific institutes, part of the Université Libre de Bruxelles (Free University of Brussels). The innovation was made possible by the sponsorship of Ernest and Alfred Solvay, fellow industrialist Raoul Warocqué, and three bankers – Georges Brugmann, Fernand Jamar and Léon Lambert. The Solvays invented a process to produce soda ash. Its manufacture proved extremely profitable as it was sold for a wide variety of industrial uses. Their company eventually expanded into the production of other alkali products, including caustic soda, salts, calcium chloride and baking soda.

The band of industrialists oversaw the placement here of Institutes for Physiology, Hygiene, Bacteriology, and Therapeutics; Anatomy and Histology; the Sociology Institute; and the School of Commerce. The Province of Brabant added the Pasteur Institute later.

The demise of academics in Leopold Park occurred in 1921 when needing more space ULB moved from the center city to the Solbosch campus further away from the city center, deciding that Leopold Park was too small to accommodate all of the academic buildings that were needed. The university's scientific institutions joined the new campus. Some of Leopold Park's buildings were demolished while others received a new assignment.

Walk counter clockwise around the pond. The building on the park's northwest corner (up the hill from the abandoned ticket kiosks) is the former home of the Institute of Hygiene. After the original building was destroyed, George Eastman of Kodak fame from Rochester, New York, built a dental clinic for poor children on the site in 1935. The Institute of Dentistry's attractive façade was designed to encourage young patients to cross the threshold.

The building now houses the House of European History. A major focus is the definition of a common European, rather than a collection of national, histories. The museum illustrates how national unrest spread revolution across Europe; how Europe's economic power allowed it to colonize much of the world; how alliances tore Europe apart leading to world war; and how common bonds gave birth to united Europe starting with steel and coal agreements needed for reconstruction after World War II.

Mostly out of sight further up the hill are the buildings of the former Brabant Pasteur Institute where important discoveries were made in the study of immunity.

The building next to the Eastman Institute housed the Institute of Physiology. Cartouches bear the names of great scientists on the walls. Reflecting the common belief of the time that air and light were required to stay healthy, the building's architect made extensive use of iron and glass. Today, the building is used as a high school.

Next is the Business School. Two reliefs depict trade and travel, requirements for the commerce that marked the Belgian economy at the turn of the last century. Four delicate chimneys are the buildings' most notable characteristic. It is now part of the high school.

The white building you walked past on the way to the pond is the crown jewel of the park. The Solvay Library was inaugurated in 1902 in the building of the Institute for Sociology. Sociologist Emile Waxweiler was asked how the building should be organized in light of the new theories on academic teaching. His solution was to place the library at the center of the floor plan surrounding it with numerous studies designed to encourage students and teachers to reflect individually and to learn through emulation. Unlike the other buildings which featured iron and glass, stone was the chief building characteristic of the Institute for Sociology, selected to protect the students from distractions. The crown of the roof and chimneys, however, pay tribute to the Art Nouveau style of the day.

For a time after the ULB move to the Solbosch campus, the library was home to the university press, but in 1981 the building was abandoned. Ten years later, renovation began to restore the building's rich architectural heritage, including the magnificent basilica-shaped reading room.

Atop the hill to the left is the Museum of the Royal Institute of Natural Science. There are three distinguishable buildings that form the complex. The former convent of the Redemptorist Ladies acquired by the Society of Zoology in 1860 is the low building. The south wing behind it was built between 1891 and 1905 in an institutional design for museums typical for the time. The tall building was designed in the early 1930s but not constructed until the 50s.

Continuing counter clockwise, hidden behind a playground at the bottom of the hill is the Eggevoort tower dating from the 15th Century, a last vestige of the Medieval estates in the area. It served as a small hunting lodge when it was built.

The last of the park's scientific institutions is the Institute of Anatomy built in 1893 by architect Jules-Jacques Van Ysendyck in collaboration with engineer Leon Gerard. The cartouches in sgraffito are reminders of Raoul Warocque, founder of the institute and defender of secular and liberal ideas.

You are at the southeast corner of Leopold Park. Exit diagonally across from where you entered, crossing rue de Malebeek and walking through Place Jourdan.

Point 8: Maison Antoine

In the center of Place Jourdan is what is called the best friterie in Brussels, Maison Antoine. It dates from 1948 when Antoine Desmet opened his stand in a shack left behind by the Germans when they fled Brussels at the end of World War II. Unfortunately, the shack was replaced in 2017 by a new stand.

Here frites are not the side order. In a friterie they are the star of the show, with hamburgers and sausages as optional side orders. Since it is Belgium, escargots are also available.

Maison Antoine follows the Belgian tradition of cooking frites twice, once at a low temperature and then fried a second time at a high temperature when ordered to add the golden-brown color and crispiness. Maison Antoine offers about a dozen sauces as alternatives to the Belgian tradition of mayonnaise. Americans often take the cocktail, which combines ketchup and mayonnaise for a Belgian twist on the American preference.

After successfully navigating the friterie experience, it is time to sit, enjoy the frites nestled in their paper wrapper container, and select an appropriate beer as a companion. Be forewarned. The frites are very hot when served.

Stop 9: Chez Bernard or Bistrot le Jourdan

If a bar or cafe surrounding Place Jourdan displays the sign of a smiling frites container, you are welcome to sit with your frites and order a beverage. Two of these on the western side of the square are Chez Bernard and Bistrot le Jourdan.

Chez Bernard is a local hangout with tables outside, a mirrored wall inside, and a garden conservatory in the back. One choice here is the Rodenbach Original, a beer often on draft from western Flanders. Its brown coloring is gained from aging in oak casks for two years. Another is the Bush Ambree, first brewed in 1933. The Bush Ambrée contains only malt, hops, natural sugars, and water drawn from the well beneath the brewery. The high density of the malt in the wort and the house yeast with its unique flavoring push the alcohol volume up to 12%, making it one of the strongest beers in Belgium. The brewery promotes Bush Ambree as a digestive (and an aperitif too).

Despite its high alcohol content, Bush can still be called an "amber-bier," the classic Belgian beer style (also called "spéciale belge"), dating from the beginning of the 20th-century. That's when the Belgische Brouwers (Federation of Belgian Brewers) held "A Contest for the Improvement of Belgian Beer." The aim was to compete with the pils beers from abroad that were then flooding the Belgian market. The spéciale belge was the result, designed to be a drinkable alternative to pils. The beer style is rooted in the Belgian tradition of high fermentation beers, top-fermented beers, but balancing hop, malt and yeast more equally.

Boulettes (meatballs and frites) are a traditional Belgian lunch dish. They are traditionally served with a tomato sauce. If you would like to try the Flemish take, Bistrot le Jourdan, a few doors away from Chez Bernard, is the place to visit. The meatballs, known as Boulettes à la Liégeoise, are served in a velvety brown sauce. Adding sugar is an important step, the chef says. Try them with Charles Quint, a beer named for a 16th Century emperor of the Holy Roman Empire.

Beers Bank on the southeast corner of the square is a new addition which does not have the local feel of Chez Bernard or the boulettes of Bistrot le Jourdan but does have beer choices on two floors.

Return: Go to the northeast end of Place Jourdan (the end opposite Maison Antoine). Walk up the hill along rue Froissart for four blocks where you will reach the Schuman Roundabout. Hop on the Metro to center city.

Walk 6
St. Catherine's

The Old Harbor

**Length of Walk: 1 hour
without museums or debrief**

Connecting Dots: In the 16th Century, basins were built adjacent to the River Senne north of Grand Place creating a thriving harbor and fish market. As the river became polluted, the market could no longer be supported. With the covering of the Senne in the mid-19th Century to improve living conditions in the Lower Town, much of the area's Medieval character was lost. Warehouses, some incorporating the characteristics of Art Nouveau, replaced houses and small shops near the old harbor. What remained of the ancient housing and commerce was further destroyed by construction that linked the north and south railway stations. Planning for the connection began in 1909, but it was not until 1952 that Brussels Central Station opened on the new line. Other 20th Century urban development added blocks of drab office buildings sucking life from the area.

Starting Point: Entrance to the Metro at St. Catherine in the center of the Marche aux Poissons.

Point 1: Marche aux Poissons

When you step out of the Metro at St. Catherine, you are in the middle of Brussels' old harbor and fish market.

Beginning in 1561 when the Willebroeck Canal opened to connect the Senne River to the River

Walk 6 Map 1

Scheldt and the North Sea, the area thrived. Quays were built for the unloading and selling of goods. Residents came to buy fresh fish.

All that was to change. The river became too polluted to support fishing. More sewer than body of water, the river became a health hazard. In the mid-19th Century, the city covered it. All but one of the basins were filled, and the area's Medieval housing was destroyed. The 1922 opening of a canal to the northwest dealt the final blow to St. Catherine's as the city harbor. Today, only the street names keep alive the memory of the quays and Medieval life: Briques (bricks), Bois a Brulon (firewood), Houille (coal) and Foin (hay) among them.

Point 2: Anspach Monument

Walk away from the church down Marche aux Poissons along Quai aux Briques. Stop on the left side at the mid-point of the furthest basin. An obelisk-fountain topped by who else, St. Michael, the patron saint of Brussels, will be on your right, emerging from the water. This is the Anspach Monument dedicated to 19th Century

Mayor Jules Anspach, champion of urban development to benefit the working class. Constructed in 1897, it has only been in St. Catherine's since 1981. It was originally the center piece of Place de Brouckere before it was put into storage in 1973 when the Metro line was built there.

About six blocks to the west (in the direction away from the church) is Canal de Charleroi where the Senne still flows. Built from 1827 to 1832, the north south waterway allowed coal to be transported from the mines in southern Belgium to Brussels and then through connecting canals to Antwerp and other cities, fueling the industrial revolution and enabling Belgium to assume a commanding manu-facturing position in pre-World War I Europe.

With the opening of the canal in 1832, the portion of the Senne flowing through the center city near Grand Place was no longer needed for navigation. Because the river was polluted, a health hazard, and an eye sore anyway, it was covered in 1871 as part of a major urban development project to beautify and modernize Brussels.

Point 3: No. 46 rue de Flandre

Continue to the end of the fountain, follow the road as it bends left, then go left onto Marche aux Porcs. After one block go left again onto rue de Flandre.

This crowded street in today's Brussels became a main artery beginning in the 11th Century. Part of the ancient east-west trade route through Brussels, rue de Flandre was one of the city's first paved roads. Some of its buildings date from the 17th Century.

Stop at Number 46 and walk inside. Down a hallway is the covered courtyard of La Maison La Bellone, its name taken from a Roman goddess whose bust stands in the middle. Designed by architect Jean Coslyn, the courtyard was built between 1697 and 1708 to serve a 17th Century stone house which still stands. The façade plays upon the numbers 7 and 12.

Point 4: Daringman

At No. 37 rue de Flandre is a laid-back Flemish pub. The ambiance is that of a coffee shop. Customers engage in serious discussion with newspapers strewn about. Since there is no set beer list, ask your server for a recommendation. One choice might be Gageleer, what is called a "sustainable" beer. Around 1980, the founders had a vision to brew a beer for Medieval tastes. Their quest led them to the Cruydeboeck ("Book of Herbs") by Belgian botanist and physician Rembert Dodoens (1517-1585) and eventually to what they called their "garage beer." In 2003, the beer was certified as organic. If Gageleer is not available or if you want a non-organic choice, ask for a Flemish ale.

Continue along rue de Flandre. You will soon be in the plaza in front of the church that gives its name to the area.

Point 5: St. Catherine's

St. Catherine's was built in the 14th and 15th Centuries. All that remains from the original structure is the Baroque tower. Most of what is seen today was built in the 19th Century during the time the city covered the Senne. Inside is the Black Madonna statue from the 14th Century. Years of aging have turned the limestone of which the statue is made black.

A curiosity about the church is that its western side (facing Marche aux Poissons and its water-filled basins) serves as an outdoor urinal. Such urinals were introduced in Brussels in 1845. "Outdoor" urinals in frequently traveled places helped acquaint the populace with appropriate hygiene.

Another curiosity is that it sells beer. In collaboration with the Brussels Beer Project, not far away at 188 rue Antoine Dansaert, the church shop sells Ste Kat beer, a Belgian pale ale at 7% ABV. It is effervescent and full of life, like the church, its proponents say. Profit from sale of the beer funds church renovations.

Point 6: Shot Tower

To the right of the church is what looks like a belfry, easily identifiable by the clock on its side. The building is actually a lead shot tower. Following a process invented in 1782, lead is heated until molten. Surface tension shapes the liquid led into droplets that are dropped from a point high in the tower inside a copper sieve causing the balls to solidify. The balls are caught at the floor in a water-filled basin. An inclined table is used to check for roundness,

and different sieves are used to create shots that are of bigger or smaller sizes. The size of the shot that can be created is determined by the tower's height.

Walk along the right side of the church.

Point 7: The Black Tower

Behind the church on the right is the Black Tower, a remnant of the city's First Wall dating from the 12th Century.

Between 5,000 and 10,000 people lived in Brussels at the time of the tower's construction. The First Wall was built seven meters (23 feet) high and stretched for four kilometers (two and a half miles) around the city. It was 2.3 meters (7.5 feet) thick with seven gateways to access the city. There were fifty towers with the Black Tower one of them. It protected the city from invaders approaching from the harbor.

The construction of Brussels' Second Wall eventually made the First Wall and its towers irrelevant. In the 16th Century the tower was turned into housing, and eventually it became completely concealed by buildings. The tower was rediscovered and rescued from demolition by the Mayor Charles Buls at the end of the 19th Century.

To immediately start Walk 7, continue walking away from the church, turning right onto rue de l'Eveque. Stop when you reach Boulevard Anspach, turn left and stand outside the Hotel Metropole. Walk 7 begins at Place de Brouckeree.

If instead you would like a debrief in St. Catherine's and leave Walk 7 for another time, return to the front of the church, walk to the far end of Place Sainte Catherine, turn left onto rue Sainte Catherine.

Point 8: Monk

Debrief. Found on the right side of the street, patrons like Monk for its laid back atmosphere in the day and bustle at night.

Among the beers on tap is Cristal, a light regional pils. If you would like a stronger beer, try La Trappe's Quadrupel. It is a 10% amber colored ale with a smooth finish. The beer continues to ferment after bottling. La Trappe does not qualify for our Belgian beer checklist because the abbey from which it is brewed is in The Netherlands.

For a snack, Monk offers sausage or cheese. For lunch or dinner, visit La Villette. Exit Monk and turn left stopping at the first street. The restaurant at No. 3 rue du Vieux Marché aux serves traditional Belgian dishes, many cooked in beer, and has more than forty Belgian beer selections.

Return by walking to the Metro at St. Catherine. Grand Place is also only a short walk away.

Walk 7
Place de Brouckere

City Lights

Length of Walk: 1.5 hours
without museums or debrief
Museum Options: Comic Strip Center •
Museum of Original Figurines

Connecting Dots: Prior to the 19th Century, north of the old harbor hosted craft shops, tanneries, breweries, other small industries, and squalid housing. The covering of the Senne gave birth to a new city center, one made especially for the urban life style of late 19th Century. To distinguish it from other sections of Brussels, buildings around the square were built of stone, a deviation from the norm of brick construction in the Belgian capital. Shaped by the new technologies of electric lights, electrified street cars, and most importantly the moving picture, Place de Brouckere was the place for residents to be seen and was the favored destination for visitors. Changing tastes and ill-advised urban development ultimately led to de Brouckere's losing its luster. Too many cars, too many hotels in other parts of the city, and changing tastes made a night at the cinema center not what it used to be. Perhaps yet another transformation can restore its prominence.

Starting Point: Entrance to the Metro at Place de Brouckere in front of Hotel Metropole.

Point 1: Place de Brouckere

You can pause here to connect the dots of Brussel's history or, as recommended, read this section while

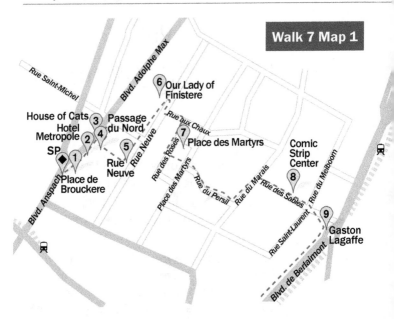

Walk 7 Map 1

sitting in the Hotel Metropole Café, on the eastern or right side of Place de Brouckere.

Prior to the 19th Century, this area was home to craft shops, tanneries, breweries, other small industries, and even more so to squalid housing. The River Senne often overflowed, becoming a muddy sewer. There were no open spaces, only tangled alleyways nearly 200 of which were dead ends. There was no running water, and an average of more than 200 people shared each latrine. Cholera periodically decimated the population.

Brussels Mayor Jules Anspach demanded that as part of the 1867 to 1871 project to cover the Senne, slums be eradicated and replaced by improved housing. Grand boulevards allowing for horse drawn trams and later electric trams to move between the city's train stations and other destinations were part of his vision. He believed urban beautification and social activism needed to work hand in hand. His goal was nothing less than to make Brussels the grandest of European capitals while improving the social condition of its inhabitants.

He shared that goal with King Leopold II, at least the beautification part. While the king focused on adding grandeur to the Upper Town and the communes outside the city proper, Anspach kept his attention on improving the Lower Town. He believed a new city center with modern conveniences was essential to keep and attract the growing number of prosperous businessmen profiting from Belgium's industrialization. Their presence would support the commerce on which the working class depended for employment. The reality was that the beautification projects pushed the city's poor into other depressed areas of the city making them more crowded. Many of the displaced found their way to Anderlecht, an industrial area southwest of the city center.

The centerpiece of Anspach's vision was Place de Brouckere. Its design, the work of Léon Suys, copied the style of Haussman, the architect who transformed Paris with grand boulevards lined by large hotels, impressive apartment houses, fashionable shops and department stores. Brussels would now have the same. To distinguish the square from other sections of Brussels, Suys used stone, a deviation from the Belgian capital's norm of brick construction. The facades on the western side of Boulevard Anspach illustrate the revival Flemish Neo-Renaissance style popular in the late 19th Century. The buildings' flamboyant style creates a harmony because of their similar proportions.

When the vaulting of the Senne was completed in 1871, two main boulevards split off from the main avenue heading north. Sitting at the juncture was the former Church of the Augustinians, part of a convent founded in 1336 that included on its western side gardens, a bakery and brewery. When the Augustinian Friars were expelled from the city after the French revolution, the convent buildings were converted to hospitals. Soldiers who fought in the Battle of Waterloo in 1815 were treated here. During the Revolution of 1830, Belgian patriots lived on the grounds. After de-consecration in 1842, the church building itself first became a concert hall, then a theater, and finally a post office.

One of the northward bound avenues cut through the former convent's gardens. The other avenue, the one to the right, ended at the north train station, Gare du Nord, its roof visible from Place de Brouckere. Suys used the former church as a focal point for his design of the square, preserving it at great expense since the work to cover the river nearly surrounded the church.

In 1874, the Continental Hotel opened in back of the church between the two avenues. It was the stateliest hotel in the city, known for its richly decorated tavern and large outdoor terrace on the ground floor. The roof line of the old hotel, though altered after a 1901 fire, can be seen on the western boulevard, Boulevard Émile Jacqmain.

Eventually the old church building became more obstacle than focal point. In 1893, the city demolished all but its façade, the church's presence unsuitable for the increasing tram and pedestrian traffic that flowed here. The Italian-Flemish renaissance facade dating from 1642, disassembled brick by brick, lives on as the façade of the St. Trinity Church in Ixelles.

The square's new focal point became the entrance of the Continental Hotel with its architectural style modeled after The Louvre. The building seen today in the middle of the square is the former entrance to the hotel.

At the place where the church was in the square, the city constructed a fountain as a memorial to Mayor Anspach. When the city constructed the entrance to the Metro station beneath the square in 1973, the Anspach obelisk fountain was dismantled. After a stint in storage, it was moved to where it resides now, in the old fish market.

While the setting of Place de Brouckere was grand with people meeting here from far and wide, there was one problem. Prosperous businessmen chose not to live here. Rather than living in apartment houses, they preferred housing to the north in Schaerbeek, the former location of the farms that supplied the breweries with the cherries for kriek beer, or to the east in the Leopold Quarter, the Royals' old hunting grounds. The appeal of green space and town mansions over flats was too great.

Still Place de Brouckere was the center of Brussels nightlife as Belgian singer Jacques Brel evoked in a 1962 song when he described how here "we saw windows, men with women in crinoline" during the city's Belle Époque period in the early 20th Century.

As cinemas became the rage in European cities, in Brussels they found their home in Place de Brouckere and the surrounding streets. With movie marquis and electric signs seemingly everywhere, the place had the feel of Times Square in New York or London's Piccadilly Circus.

Le Théâtre du cinématographe, said to be the first building constructed for the viewing of cinema, opened in 1904 in a location a little further up on the Boulevard Adolphe Max, the right fork in the road. Also on Boulevard Adolphe Max, the Plaza and Marivaux cinemas, now incorporated into hotels, drew huge crowds. Nearby on rue de Malines, the now abandoned Variétés became in 1937 the first cinema to have neon lights. One block to the east, a dozen cinemas were on Rue Neuve, a street known for dance halls, ice cream parlors, tea rooms and bars.

Directly across from the Hotel Metropole, the first movie house in the square opened in 1915 as American Cinema, later renamed Cinema des Princes. It was one of the biggest ever built in Belgium, seating 2,705 and featuring modern features like elevators and air conditioning. The Art Deco style auditorium was inspired by African art. The foyer was in the International Modern style with cubist decorative panels.

Much of the Princes was demolished in 1932 before reopening as the Eldorado Cinema. Although the theater has undergone several more expansions and renovations, Screen 7 "The Eldorado" pays homage to the theater's early 20th Century roots, retaining the original woodwork.

Place de Brouckere reached its peak of popularity in the late 1950s with the installation of a tourist information center for the 1958 World Expo hosted by Brussels. The modern building with its light-weight, transparent appearance and sweeping roofline was so popular it remained open long after the Expo closed.

While still busy, Place de Brouckere has lost its luster. In the 1960s developers began to let older buildings deteriorate so new ones could be built in their place. Pedestrian unfriendly buildings, far from supporting the character of the square, appeared at the southern end. Construction of the Metro under the square from 1969 to 1976 further disfigured it. The central esplanade lost its shape due to the four-lane highway built around it making the square unrecognizable to an early mid-20th Century visitor except for the front of the old Continental Hotel. The latest renovation of Place de Brouckere aims at eliminating auto traffic and making it once again pedestrian friendly. Readers of this book after its publication will know the success of the effort.

Point 2: Hotel Metropole

In 1890, two brothers who owned a brewery in the area opened the Cafe Metropole. Their strategy was simple. Serve the overflow crowd from the Continental Hotel. By 1895, the cafe expanded into the bank next door and opened as a hotel. If you look at the hotel's reception desk, you can see it is from the former bank building.

The hotel was a modern novel of the time, with electricity and central heating. Take a look inside to view the Corinthian columns and the other ornate features. Meeting rooms are decorated in a Renaissance style. In 1911, the hotel hosted the first Solvay Conference on Physics attended by Albert Einstein, Ernest Solvay, Ernest Rutherford, Max Planck, Marie Curie, among others. In 1949 the Metropole's barman invented the Black Russian cocktail for the United States ambassador to Luxembourg.

Point 3: House of Cats

Go right from the Hotel Metropole walking along Boulevard Adolphe Max. Passage du Nord is a few steps away. Before you enter, look at No. 1, the building to the left of the passage.

The avenues created as part of the project to vault the Senne – Hainaut Boulevard (now Maurice Lemonnier Boulevard south of the Bourse), Central Boulevard (now Boulevard Anspach), North Boulevard (now Adolphe Max Boulevard), and Senne Boulevard (now Émile Jacqmain Boulevard) – opened to traffic from 1871 to 1873. The construction of private buildings lining them continued long after because of lack of demand. Land was expensive due to the large construction costs of the vaulting, and affluent residents were not convinced settling in center city afforded the life style they desired.

To spur development, the city gave builders an incentive to create elaborate and appealing facades by arranging an architectural competition. Twenty buildings built before January 1, 1876 would be eligible to win prizes. The first prize of 20,000 francs was awarded to Henri Beyaert who designed No. 1 "Hier ist in den kater en de kat" ("House of Cats"). The competition helped, but it was not until 1895 that all the real estate lining the boulevards around Place de Brouckere was filled.

Next door at No. 3 stands the Art Deco Hotel Atlanta designed by architect Michel Polak. It was one of three hotels designed by Polak in the 1920s along the avenue connecting Place de Brouckere with the Place Rogier near Gare du Nord to accommodate visitors to the 1930 international exhibitions in Liege and Antwerp.

Walk down the "gallery street" Passage du Nord to your right.

Point 4: Passage du Nord

Gallery streets were common in European cities of the 19th Century Europe. Between 1820 and 1860, ten arcades were built in Brussels. Besides Passage du Nord, two others survive: Royal St Hubert Arcade, near Grand Place, and the Bortier Arcade, built in 1847 just to the south of today's Central Station. Passage du Nord, actually a six-story building 70 meters (230 feet) long and six meters (twenty feet) wide covering over 5,000 square meters (54,000 square feet), opened in 1882. Its shopping arcade was designed in typical 19th Century eclectic style.

The use of sculpture on such a large scale bears witness to the sense of luxury the developers wanted to convey. On the Boulevard Adolph Max façade, four groups of children, sculpted by Albert Desenfans, hold candelabras topped with lanterns. One is an allegory of recreation and the other of meditation. Four series of caryatids, sculpted by Joseph Bertheux, of the same eight designs support the glass roof. Their poses and attributes make allusions to metallurgy, commerce, the navy, astronomy, architecture, sculpture, painting and the decorative arts.

The passage opened with some 30 shops, a winter garden, children's theater, restaurant, concert hall, gaming room, laboratory for performing chemistry and physics experiments, and a museum with galleries for exhibitions of industrial products, modern inventions, works of art, curiosities and antiques.

Today, the ground floor contains only 20 shops as several of the old shops were brought together to form larger premises. The space occupied by the museum is now part of the Hotel Metropole and has been converted into meeting rooms and guest bedrooms. The only remaining traces of the museum are the two signs advertising the "Musée du Nord" on the building's Boulevard Adolphe Max façade. Admission to the museum cost one Belgian franc.

Point 5: rue Neuve

Exit Passage du Nord at rue Neuve, the second business pedestrian walking street in Belgium. Turn left.

Laid out in 1617, it was originally named rue Notre Dame for the ancient church located on the street. In the 1700s and early 1800s, this was the wealthiest section in the Lower Town. Mansions lined the street. Before construction of the boulevards as part of the vaulting of the Senne, the street served as the main connection between the north and south railway stations. Fine hotels were situated here catering to the influx of English tourists who came to Brussels on the way to Waterloo to see the battlefield where Wellington earned his greatest victory. The street was home to Brussels' first department store, and the first tram ran along it. In 1932 one of the grand movie houses opened here, the Metropole.

A true palace for cinema, the Metropole was designed by the architect Adrien Blomme for the Wielemans family in a style reminiscent of an ocean liner. It sat up to 3,000 people. If you look at the entrance to the Zara department store, you will be able to make out the covered entrance to the former theater.

In 1976, Rue Neuve became a pedestrian street.

Point 6: Our Lady of Finistere

Pass two streets as you walk along rue Neuve. Our Lady of Finistere will be on the left. Today's church, built at the beginning of the 18th Century and later restored, replaced a 17th Century church that was built on the spot of an old chapel located at the extreme limit of Brussels during the Middle Ages. Today's church is a mix of baroque with abundant and lavish internal decoration in classical styles. It also contains many works of art from the 16th to 18th Centuries. The church chapel is said to provide good luck to students visiting to study for examinations dating from the time when the University of Brussels was located where the Central Station is today.

Cross rue Neuve going away from the church along rue aux Chaux. The intersection is across from the church. The first street on the right is rue des Roses. Walk into the square.

Point 7: Place des Matryes

In the Middle Ages, drapers used the land here to spread out their cloth for drying and bleaching. With the demise of the cloth trade in the 18th Century, the city bought the land and commissioned the design of the Neoclassical square. Named place Saint-Michel when the square opened, the name was later changed to Place des Matryes to commemorate those who died during the Belgian revolution of 1830.

The statue in the center represents the motherland with the Belgian lion at her feet. The base of the monument details the events of the revolution and lists the 445 people who lost their lives.

Walk diagonally across the square, exiting in the middle of the eastern side at rue de Persil. Follow that to Rue de Marais where it ends turning left. You will walk through a cavern of unremarkable office buildings that sapped the vitality from the area in the mid-20th Century. After one block turn right onto rue des Sables.

Point 8: Comic Strip Center

What do the Smurfs, Blake and Mortimer, Sirou and Fantasio, and Tintin have in common? They were created by Belgians. They and hundreds of other comic strip characters hold special places at the Belgian Comic Strip Center. The museum will be on the left side of rue des Sables.

First, we need to look at the building. The Comic Strip Center is in the former Waucquez Warehouse, an Art Nouveau creation of Victor Horta from 1906. The Waucquez family used the building for their cloth wholesale business. A glass ceiling fills a central hall with sunlight, providing the warehouse with natural light, a trademark of Art Nouveau. The building was left abandoned before being restored from 1987 to 1989 to accommodate the Comic Strip Center.

Belgium has been identified with the comic strip, the so called "ninth art," since the 1920s largely due to Herge, the creator of the character Tintin in 1929. The Comic Strip Center possess works by some 700 Belgian comic strip artists, giving Belgium the title of most comic strip artists per square kilometer of any country in the world. In fact, comic strips are so much a part of the Belgian psyche, Belgium has four comic strip museums. Most well-known European comic strip artists have studied at some time during their careers in Belgium. And if you need a reminder about how the comic strip is embedded in the Brussels psyche, simply walk around the Lower Town to see murals on the sides of buildings depicting the most famous of Belgium's comic strip characters.

The Comic Strip Center shows the evolution of European comic books beginning in 1929 and takes the visitor on a behind the scenes look at how a comic strip is created. The center makes more than 40,000 titles are available for reference and displays original comic artwork and memorabilia. Ask for the English language museum guide since most of the descriptions are in French and Flemish.

Before departing, stop in the center's café. There you can enjoy a Nero Bier. The Nero character was created by Marc Sleen, recognized in the Guinness Book of World Records as the most prolific comic strip artist. Nero is a good hearted every man, lazy and always in trouble. In the first Nero strip in 1947, Sleen creates a criminal who uses beer to brainwash Belgians into doing his bidding. In a subsequent adventure, Nero discovers a beer tree in Rwanda which makes him rich. In real life, Nero Bier is a cloudy amber ale more hoppy than other Belgian ales that is especially brewed for the center.

Leave the museum and turn left. Cross rue du Meiboom and up the stairs to Boulevard de Berlaimont. Gaston awaits at the top.

Point 9: Statue of Gaston Lagaffe and North South Rail Link

The comic strip character Gaston first appeared in 1957, a creation of the Belgian cartoonist Andre Franquin. Gaston is a lazy and accident-prone office worker whose surname translates to "the blunder."

Turn right walking past the National Bank of Belgium on the other side of Boulevard Berlaimont.

The sterile environment you are walking through results from the destruction of neighborhoods when Brussels' north and south rail stations were linked in the 20th Century. Some 1,200 homes were leveled along the three-kilometer (two-mile) route.

An underground rail connection between the stations was considered in the 1860s as part of the plan to cover the Senne. At the time, the stations were connected by a single track running along the boulevards that replaced the First Medieval Wall.

In 1909, a law was passed requiring a direct connection, and in 1910 Victor Horta was awarded the design of the Central Station building complex to serve as a transportation hub between the two stations. He completed the design in 1912, and the destruction of Brussels' Putterie district soon followed. Residents and businesses were displaced.

Decades of stop and go construction came next. The First World War sapped Belgium's resources, and after the war, financial constraints made progress minimal. Between 1927 and 1935, work was suspended only to be interrupted when it began again by World War II. The swath of land between the north and south stations was filled with debris and void of development until the Central Station and the underground rail link finally opened in 1952.

At the corner of rue d'Assaut, you will see a cathedral on your left.

Point 10: Cathederale des St-Michel et St-Gudule

Construction on the cathedral began in the 13th Century under orders from Henry 1, Duke of Brabant, and took about 300 years to complete. During my walks to write this book, some office buildings constructed in Brussels seemed to have taken that long. The Gothic style was typical of the time. The cathedral sits atop the remnants of a Romanesque church from the 11th Century.

On the columns inside are statues of the apostles, Baroque style works from the 17th Century. They were built after the church was sacked by iconoclasts who challenged the teachings of the church in the 16th Century to emphasize the apostolic origin of the church. The pillars of the church are decorated with curled row-foliage cabbage leaves linked by crosswise ribbons, typical features of the Brabantine style.

In conjunction with construction of the North-South railway junction, a Romanesque "Westbau" from 1047 was discovered. A "Westbau" is a projecting part of the construction on the west side of Romanesque churches which served as fortified refuge for the people in

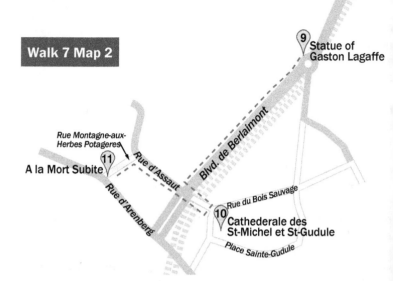

the Middle Ages. Mirrors provide viewing of the "Westbau" and the entrance to the Romanesque church. The traces of the outside walls and other features of the church have been indicated with lighter-colored flagstones. The pavement of the Romanesque church is about 1.7 meters (5.5 feet) below the level of the existing Gothic church. The foundations of the Romanesque church were used as a burial place during the Gothic period.

A notable feature of the cathedral is its great organ sitting in its "bird's nest" position to meet the specific needs of the acoustics of a gothic cathedral. Organs occupy similar positions in the cathedrals of Chartres, Cologne and Strasbourg. The instrument has a total of 4,300 pipes, 63 stops, 4 keyboards and the pedal-board. In the middle the organist's console is big enough to accommodate a soloist.

After leaving the cathedral, look at the northern tower. In spring, a pair of peregrine falcons return annually to mate and raise their young in the tower.

Return to the intersection of Boulevard de Berliamont. Walk away from the cathedral down rue d'Assaut for one block. Turn left onto rue Montagne-aux-Herbes Potageres. At No 7 is A la Mort Subite, the last debriefing point but not the last stop.

Point 11: A la Mort Subite

At the turn of the last century, young workers at the Bank of Belgium played a drinking game called 421. The player who lost the last game before returning to work was called Mort Subite or the sudden death. In 1928 the owner of the pub where the game was played moved to this location, appropriating the name. A la Mort Subite retains the original decor from 1928. How can you not have a Mort Subite Gueuze beer here? It has very little head and no bitterness.

Return: You should be able to find the Central Station Metro if 421 has not disabled you.

An interesting way to enter the station and to add two more visits is to exit A la Mort Subite turning left. At rue d'Arenberg turn left again. Turn right onto rue de la Montagne and walk two blocks. Turn left on rue du Marché aux Herbes following it past the gated entrance to Place d'Espagne where Don Quixote and his servant Sanch Panza can be found on horseback along with a memorial dedicated to Hungarian composer Bela Bartok.

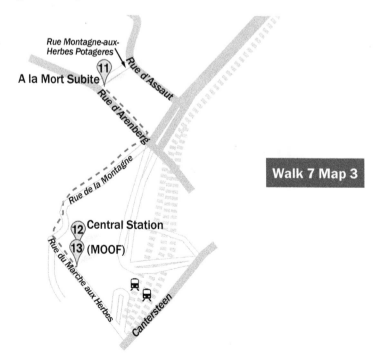

Walk 7 Map 3

If you are still on track, a Smurf statue will be in front of you. He guards the entrance to the Horta Gallery of the Central Station and the Museum of Original Figurines (MOOF).

Walk past the statue into the atrium of the Horta Gallery.

Point 12: Central Station

When standing outside the Central Station looking towards the Grand Place you would never guess that underneath lies a huge gallery designed by Victor Horta. Refurbished wooden escalators take visitors to the train platforms and main hall. This is the Horta design that he completed in 1912 but was not constructed until mid-century.

Point 13: Museum of Original Figurines (MOOF)

Return to the entrance of the gallery to visit MOOF. The museum displays more than 650 figurines and original objects selected from among the 3,500 pieces of one of the finest collections of comic book memorabilia in the world.

Now it really is time to return. The Metro is at the opposite end of the station.

Walk 8
Ixelles

Art Nouveau

**Length of Walk: 2.5 hours
without museums or debriefs**
(Take care to start about 1 PM to arrive at the Horta Museum before it closes and at the concluding Debriefing Point after it opens at 4 PM.)
Museum Options: Horta Museum

Connecting Dots: At the turn of the 19th Century, Brussels went through a period of effervescence. Belgium fueled the industrialization of continental Europe. Mines in the south provided coal and iron. The Belgian Congo provided rubber. Policies of a liberal government fostered a free spirit. Their combination yielded commercial success. At the center was Brussels. With King Leopold II beautifying the city through the construction of grand boulevards which eased transportation, former outlying areas like Ixelles, Schaerbeek and Saint-Gilles became neighborhoods and home to a growing population of successful businessmen and their families looking for a distinctive housing style to set them apart from their neighbors. Artists flocked to Brussels. In this environment of wealth and imagination, Art Nouveau, architecture's "Modern Style," was launched in 1893 by Victor Horta and Paul Hankar.

Starting Point: Exit the Metro at Louise and walk on the right side of Avenue Louise away from the gold-domed Palace of Justice. After passing a few blocks with upscale shopping, you will come to the Place Stephanie roundabout. Follow Louise and the roundabout on the right-side crossing

Chaussee de Charleroi. Cross Louise to stand in the median in the middle of the avenue.

Point 1: Avenue Louise at Place Stephanie

Look west, back toward the city center.

In the early 19th Century, the eastern-bound avenue emerging from the north-south boulevard was an extension of upscale commercial activity.

In 1841, two landowners built a square at the intersection of this eastern avenue and Chaussee de Charleroi that would be suitable for Brussels' elite to partake in Sunday strolls. By 1850, 18 elegant town homes had been built around the square and along the little stretch of avenue. The square was later renamed Place Stephanie for Leopold II's youngest daughter who one day would become the crown princess of Austria through marriage into the Hapsburg dynasty.

Turn your attention to the east down Avenue Louise, away from the city center.

The section of Avenue Louise beginning near Place Stephanie was commissioned by King Leopold II in 1847 to connect the city of Brussels with a planned recreation area in Foret de Soignes. Fierce resistance from the Commune of Ixelles, however, delayed the project until 1864 when the city of Brussels finally annexed the land needed to build the avenue.

Leopold II's vision for Brussels was taking shape. The avenue followed the Haussmann design for grand boulevards that transformed Paris, serving as the core of a wealthy residential area and providing a transportation corridor for horses and carriages to reach the newly created recreation area, Bois de la Cambre.

Construction of town mansions quickly followed the avenue's opening. By the turn of the 20th Century, a double row of chestnut trees had been planted, and in the early 1900s the avenue was reconfigured to include a tram line on one side leaving a path for carriages on the other. The middle was reserved for walking until that space was used for automobile traffic. In the 1930s apartment buildings began appearing along the avenue.

The disfiguration we see today was created by preparations for the 1958 World's Fair. Underpasses for automobile traffic were added to the avenue, perhaps making driving to and from the city easier but destroying neighborhood cohesion and the elegant atmosphere leading to the Bois de la Cambre.

Return to the south side of Avenue Louise. If you noticed sexually graphic graffiti high on the side of a Place Stephanie building, you are not alone in wondering why it is there. This and other similar street art began appearing around the city in 2016. No one has claimed responsibility but locals suspect a well-known street artist. The city government calls them "inappropriate," and they may be gone by the time you read this.

Hop on the 93 or 94 Tram, exiting at Bailli, the first stop, to pick up the tour at Point 4. Alternatively, you can walk a few blocks to see two Art Nouveau residences.

If you choose to walk, continue away from the city center. At the third block, turn right onto rue de Florence.

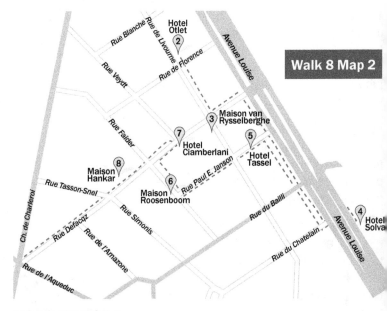

Point 2: Hotel Otlet

Number 13 rue de Florence on the corner of rue de Livourne is Hotel Otlet, built in 1894 by architect Octave van Rysselberghe. Henry van de Velde designed the interior decoration. The building was the home of Paul Marie Ghislain Otlet (1868–1944), an author, entrepreneur, lawyer and peace activist. Otlet, a Brussels native, is considered the father of information science and some say laid the foundation of the Internet. In 1905, he and Henri La Fontaine published the "Brussels Expansion," an enhancement of Dewey's classification system for books, periodicals and proceedings. It is still in use today. In 1910, Otlet founded the Central Office of National Associations, a forerunner of the League of Nations, in an effort to promote world peace.

The building is known for its gentle, aesthetic design and the stained-glass transom above the entry door.

Turn left walking along rue de Livourne, just past the first block, rue Defacqz. On the right is No. 83.

Point 3: Maison van Rysselberghe

At No. 83 is the former home of the architect Octave van Rysselberghe. Van Rysselberghe was born in Antwerp in 1855 and died in

Nice in 1929. The house was built by the architect for his own use in an eclectic style inspired by Art Nouveau.

Return to rue Defacqz and turn right towards Avenue Louise. Turn right at Louise. At the third street, rue du Chatelain, cross Louise. Turn to the right, stopping at No. 224.

Point 4: Hotel Solvay

If you took the tram from Point 1, you exited at the second stop, Bailli. Continue walking along Louise, crossing it at rue du Chatelain, the third street.

In French, "hotel" has traditionally referred to a grand townhouse. The Victor Horta designed Hotel Solvay at No. 224 Avenue Louise (notice the style of the "4" in the street address) is one of the great examples of Art Nouveau style, inside and out. Armand Solvay, the son of the wealthy Belgian chemist and industrialist Ernest Solvay, commissioned the work in the 1894, instructing Horta to spare no expense in creating a beautiful residence for his bride.

Horta, relatively unknown at the time, enjoyed complete freedom and designed not just the house itself but every detail including furniture, carpets, light fixtures, and tableware. He used the most expensive materials: marble, onyx, bronze and woods from the tropics. Look at the doorbell. It too was designed by Horta. Construction began in 1895 with the last of the furnishings completed in 1903.

Horta created his designs by working from the inside out. The interior layout dictated the façade of the building. Since many houses in the Art Nouveau style were designed before the wide-spread use of electricity and addition of light fixtures, large windows were necessary to provide adequate lighting. Horta's solution was to adapt the metal frame used in industrial structures to create open, light filled interiors.

Horta's belief in the vitality of the human spirit led to designs that both inspired and offered convenience in the new urban lifestyle of the 20th Century. The curved lines visible in the exterior of the building were carried over from the decoration of the interior with its light-diffused open spaces. Among the most striking features is the central stairway for which Horta engaged a Belgian artist to create images using small, distinct dots of pure color to create images.

The current resident of Hotel Solvay is Louis Wittamer whose shop is the Official Chocolate Supplier to the Court of Belgium. You can enjoy the family's chocolates and other deserts at their cafe on the Sablon.

For the next stop, return to rue de Chatelain to cross Louise, and turn right, heading back towards center city. Turn left at the second street, rue Paul E Janson. Hotel Tassel will be on your left at No. 6 rue Paul-Emile Janson.

Point 5: Hotel Tassel

Hotel Tassel, built between 1893 and 1897 for the Belgian scientist and professor Emile Tassel, was Horta's breakthrough design, completed just before his work on Hotel Solvay. It is considered the first Art Nouveau building because of its innovative floor plan, use of materials, and decoration. The design was revolutionary in that it incorporates metal, a modern building material of the time, into residential architecture. Another modern feature is the extensive use of glass. The bow window adds light and a feeling of spaciousness to the interior. The façade uses moldings and columns to retain a connection with classical design.

Hotel Tassel has three distinct parts. Two parts are brick and stone, one facing the street and the other on the side of garden. The third part is a steel structure covered with glass that links the two and brings natural light into the house. A central garden lying underneath the glass completes the structure. Staircases with landings connect rooms and floors. The building represents one of the first uses of wrought iron in a residence.

Horta-designed residences like the Hotel Tassel were very expensive, but contemporary architects copied Horta's decorative style, giving traditionally designed residences Art Nouveau touches at reasonable prices.

Continue along rue Paul-Emile Jensen away from Louise until it ends at rue Faider.

Point 6: Maison Roosenboom

At the corner, No. 83 rue Faider, built in 1900, is the work of Albert Roosenboom, a student of Victor Horta's. Look for the artistic features of the Art Nouveau style. The sgraffito focuses on a woman's face with closed eyes, her index finger pointing to her mouth as a sign of silence. In sgraffito, the artist applies layers of plaster tinted with contrasting colors. The surface is then scratched to produce the outline of a drawing. Two children with closed eyes are on either side of the woman. Above the bay window is an exquisitely designed the wrought iron railing.

The interior is based on the traditional plan with three adjoining rooms on each floor, accentuated with works of craftsmanship such as wood paneling with built-in mirrors, a stone fireplace decorated with a sgraffito, and a wood fireplace with a background of green ceramic tiles.

The building's façade combines the two trends that characterized the Art Nouveau style in Brussels. The lower section illustrates the "floral" design and organic lines favored by Horta. Note the curve of the first floor's bay window and the curving structural details made from carved stone set into brick walls. The upper section followed the "geometric" style followed by the architect Paul Hankar.

Turn right away from rue Paul-Emile Jensen and walk along rue Faider for one block to rue Defacqz. Turn right.

Point 7: Hotel Ciamberlani

Hankar's work can be seen at No. 48 rue Defacqz. Another founding father of Art Nouveau, Paul Hankar built this house for the Belgian painter Albert Ciamberlani. Hankar was a classmate of Horta's at the Belgian Royal Academy of Beaux-Arts and began his career as a sculptor. He was known for the display of iron in his works.

The main feature of the building are the two horseshoe shaped windows on the second floor and the colorful brick work that surrounds them. A continuous balcony with wrought iron rail runs along the facade. The sgraffito on the first floor portrays the three stages of life. The second floor shows the labors of Hercules. The design was by Ciamberlani himself. Hankar's name and the date of construction are chiseled into a block of granite on the façade.

The building next door to the right is another Hankar work. No. 50 rue Defacqz, built in 1898 for the Belgian painter René Janssens, is known for its brickwork.

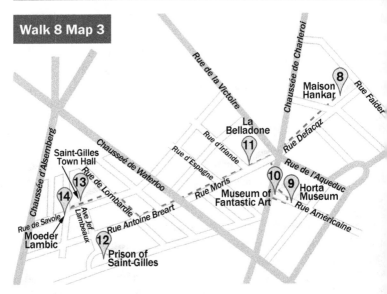

Walk 8 Map 3

Now back track. Head south, away from Avenue Louise along Rue Defacqz. No. 71 is on the right side of rue Defacqz.

Point 8: Maison Hankar

This is the studio of the architect Paul Hankar built in 1893. "P Hankar Architect" appears next to the door. Near the top of the building, panels depict morning, afternoon, evening, and night done in the sgraffito style of decoration. Hankar's preference for straight lines, rather than Horta's floral and naturalistic touches, can be seen in the bay window's rectangular glass panes.

Standing outside Hankar's studio, it is a good time to think about what distinguishes the Art Nouveau style of architecture.

Art Nouveau represented an explosion on the senses and return to nature. The movement was partly a reaction by young architects to Historicism, an architectural style of the 19th Century that reinvented the past by using old fashioned styles, usually resulting in buildings that were overbearing and pretentious. Art Nouveau was also a reaction to the monotony of mass-produced items and the escalating pace of urban life driven by new technologies. Ironically, new technologies, such as the use of metal in construction, were central to Art Nouveau design, allowing architects to open interior spaces and fill them with light.

Another feature of Art Nouveau was that buildings themselves became objects of art, both their exteriors and interiors. The growing middle class with its access to wealth and the ability of architects to marry natural materials with new production techniques enabled this transformation.

Three types of decorative styles dominated the movement: the arabesque, with its rhythmic linear patterns; floral or animal patterns; and the feminine silhouette. Forms tended to become geometric, as circles were combined with squares with greater frequency. Hundreds of houses and schools, cafés, and shops rivaled for originality. Craftsmen skilled in ironwork, wood, stained glass and mosaics added their personal stamps to projects.

The Art Nouveau period lasted from 1893 until about 1910. It is estimated that only ten percent of houses constructed during the period were true Art Nouveau in design. No one knows the exact number since so many houses have been destroyed. Also, many other houses still seen in Brussels today have the appearance of being Art Nouveau but are not true Art Nouveau designs. They might only have a single feature or two, such as wrought iron balconies or bay windows, rather than being a complete work of art designed by an architect.

Continue south along rue Defacqz until it ends at rue de l'Aqueduc. Cross rue de l'Aqueduc and then turn left onto Ch. de Charleroi. After one block, turn left on rue Americaine.

Point 9: Horta Museum

Between 1898 and 1901, Victor Horta built a studio and residence on two lots in Saint-Gilles, No. 25-26 rue Americaine. The house displays plans, photographs and architectural fragments. It is open 2 to 5:30, Tuesday to Sunday.

The mosaics, stained glass and floor plan create a harmonious whole, down to the last detail, from door hinge to landing. Horta and the other Art Nouveau architects thought of the residences they designed as decorative show places and as structures reflecting a sophisticated, elegant and technology-driven life style.

Upon entering, visitors were guided into a sitting room while servants disappeared with coats and luggage behind concealed doors.

The placement of a staircase in the center of house with the living space built around it was radical for the time. Multiple landings and a stained-glass skylight overhead provided decorative functionality. Servants had their own passages to move about without disturbing residents. Another stunning feature is an enclosed winter garden outside the kitchen with a glass covering that allowed sun to enter the entire structure.

A fundamental concept in Art Nouveau was to derive inspiration from nature. Flowers and plants were often at the center of Art Nouveau design. Instead of focusing on the flower, however, Horta chose the stem on which to base his design. Examples can be found throughout the house.

A favorite feature of the house from the man's perspective is a retractable urinal that Horta designed for next to his bed.

Exit the Horta House and turn towards Ch. de Charleroi.

Point 10: Museum of Fantastic Art

This is quirky stop, right next to the Horta House. Located in a town home, the collection focuses on everything weird and special. It balances baroque and peculiar, with all in between, always emphasizing the objects' surrealistic side. Note the museum is only open on weekend afternoons from May to September.

Walk to Ch. De Charleroi. You have serious decisions to make.

If you want to return to city center, turn right crossing rue de l'Aqueduc. The 97 Tram direction Louise can be hopped on at Ch. de Charleroi. If you want a local debrief, carry on.

Point 11: La Belladone

If it is not yet 4 PM, cross Ch. de Charleroi before reaching l'Aqueduc. Take rue Moris to the left to find La Belladone, 17A rue Moris, at the first intersection. La Belladone is a local spot, known for tea and for purposes of this book its beers on draft, including usual presences Tripel Karmeliet and Chimay.

For a unique debriefing experience that opens at 4 PM, continue walking along rue Moris away from Ch. de Charleroi, crossing rue d'Irelande and rue d'Espagne. Before crossing Ch. de Waterloo, hop onto the 81 or 97 Tram. Get off at the first stop, Lombardie, which is at the intersection of rue de Savoie. Turn left.

Points 12 and 13: Prison of Saint-Gilles and Saint-Gilles Town Hall

Walk one block along rue de Savoie. Pause at Avenue Jef Lambeaux. Look up the hill to your left to see the Prison of Saint-Gilles. The castle-like building was built between 1878 and 1884 to the concepts practiced by criminologists in the 19th Century. In World War II, the German occupational army held and tried leaders of the Belgian resistance here.

On the other side of rue de Savoie is the Saint-Gilles town hall built between 1900 and 1904 in the French Chateau style. The commune of Saint-Gilles dates to the 7th Century when the first house was built somewhere near here on the high ground overlooking the Senne river valley. If you like, step inside the town hall, going up the left staircase to see frescos by Ciamberlani. Through a door to the right is a portrait of Napoleon that once formed a panoramic painting in Paris.

Time for a beer. Continue along rue de Savoie and stop at the next intersection.

Point 14: Moeder Lambic Original

No. 68 rue de Savoie is "Mother of Lambic." It opens at 4 PM. The small bar has a continually changing assortment of lambic beers on draft. What is unique about the place is the trap door behind the bar leading to a cellar that can be reserved for tastings of beer paired with Belgian cheese.

You really should have a lambic beer. Ask the barman for a suggestion. Likely a Cantillon is available and often 3 Fonteinen, young or old lambic.

This location is the original Moeder Lambic. A sister bar is near Grand Place and is included in the Anderlecht walk.

Return: Walk back to rue de Lombardie along rue de Savoie. Get onto the 97 Tram direction Louise taking you back to center city.

Walk 9
Saint-Gilles

Applied Art in the Street

**Length of Walk: 1 hour without debriefs
Museum Options: The Halle Gate •
Porte de Halle**

Connecting Dots: Obbrussel or Upper-Brussels was settled in the 7th Century. Its high altitude provided favorable living conditions away from the marshes and crowded alleys as Brussels grew. In 1216, the nearby Forest Abbey declared Obbrussel an independent abbey. Eight years later, the City of Brussels took over administration of Obbrussel. It had grown to 41 houses. In 1670, a fort was built here to protect Brussels from invaders. In the 1700s the fort was demolished and replaced by new development and toll roads. By the end of the century, the area was named Saint-Gilles after its main church. The rural village known mainly for cabbage cultivation became a preferred area for merchants in the newly independent Belgium of the 19th Century. The population went from 2,500 around 1800 to more than 33,000 in 1880 to a peak of 60,000 in 1910. The street pattern was completely redesigned in the 1860s by architect Victor Besme to facilitate residential and commercial construction and the laying of tram lines. These were the years when the Brussels-South railway station and the new Saint Giles church were built, to be followed soon after by a new jail and city hall. Town homes emphasizing craftsmanship and distinctive touches dotted the commune. During the Secord World War, the neighborhood became a center for the resistance movement.

Starting Point: Metro Station Parvis de Saint-Gilles, a station that serves the underground trams 3, 4, 33 and 51. Take the exit marked "Parvis."

Point 1: Saint-Gilles Church

You will be thrust immediately into the plaza of Saint-Gilles Church. If you are lucky, it is Saturday morning. Merchants are selling fruits, clothing, cheeses, meats, and the occasional auto part. To the left is Saint-Gilles Church. The church building is the third to occupy the site.

The original church, built in 1216, was destroyed when the Spanish invaded the city in 1578. In 1595 a new church was erected. It served the community for a century before being destroyed by fire. It was restored in 1756. Today's church was built from 1862 to 1867 based on a Basilica and Neo-Roman design by Victor Besme, the architect who laid out the St. Gilles street grid. Organs, the church's most highly regarded feature, were added in 1878.

Next to the church is an obvious Debriefing Point.

Point 2: Brasserie Verschueren

Founded in 1880 by Louis Verschuren, the art deco design dates to a 1930 remodeling. During the Second World War, the Brasserie was a hub of Belgian resistance activity. It still has a bohemian flair. A good beer choice would be one from the West Flanders De Ranke brewery. The DeCuvée De Ranke is a mixed fermentation, blended ale, a combination of barrel-aged beer and lambic.

Return to Parvis Saint-Gilles. Walk away from the church past the Metro entrance from which you emerged earlier. Point 3 is on your right at Number 37. Stay strong. A welcoming brasserie is on the ground floor of the historic building here.

Point 3: La Maison du Peuple

The Neo-Renaissance Flemish styled People's House was designed by architect Alfred Malchair in 1905 for the Cooperative Society of Brussels, a socialist workers party. Its members volunteered for its construction.

As socialist views spread in cities throughout Europe during the early 20th Century, The People's House in St. Gilles became one of the principal places where workers' rights were debated and promoted in Brussels. In 1914, Lenin spoke here, calling for organizing "illegal cells and groups in the armies of all nations." He cited the need for a "ruthless struggle against the chauvinism and patriotism of the petty bourgeoisie and bourgeoisie of all countries without exception" and made an appeal to the "revolutionary consciousness of the toiling masses."

The large hall at the back was supported by a metal frame in the middle of a decorative Art Nouveau-style interlacing. In 1918, a cinema was added. After the Cooperative Society closed its doors in the 1960s, the space became a butcher shop, a grocery, and a church before its re-incarnation as a café.

Continue walking the full one block length of Parvis Saint-Gilles away from the church. Summon your strength again. Brasserie de L'Union is at the corner.

Head diagonally through the park to the corner of rue de l'Hotel des Monnaies and rue de la Victoire. Cross both. Your destination is No. 66 Rue de l'Hôtel des Monnaies.

Point 4: Hôtel Winssinger

Victor Horta designed this house from 1894 to 1897 for Camille Winssinger, an engineer friend of the Tassels and Solvays.

Inside are three levels plus a mezzanine. Balconies are connected to a spectacular bow window with a magnificent stairway on the inside connecting them. The interior of the house was designed to separate the reception rooms from the living quarters. As with all Horta designs, small details such as door frames and other wood-work, stained glass windows and ironwork were all integrated into the total design. Like most other homes of the day, it was not designed for electricity. Horta's high ceiling design made the most of natural lighting.

In 1928 and 1929, major renovations were made to the house. The main staircase was removed and an elevator added. More renova-tions followed, including the building's conversion into an apartment house. Recently No. 66 has undergone yet another renovation, this time to restore its original design.

Step inside the doorway. A swatch of wall paper is on the left wall. When the wall surfaces in the entry way were cleaned, the original wall paper was revealed, a floral pattern that while popular at the turn of the last century would be too much for our taste today. This gives us a hint of what decoration was like at the end of the 19th Century.

Point 5: La Forest Divonne Gallery

Tucked down the alley a part of No.66 is an art gallery that hosts exhibitions open to the public. The Brussels branch of a well-known Parisian gallery, La Forest Divonne features a "Project Room" program, dedicated to discovering young artists in addition to its usual exhibition program.

After exiting No. 66, return to the corner of de La Victoire. Cross rue de l'Hotel des Monnaies as well as rue de la Victoire. Walk downhill towards what looks like a castle. Go two blocks where you make a gentle left onto rue de la Filature. It is the road that gradually slopes downhill on your right. Walk down rue de la Filature for one block crossing Waterloo. The street is now named rue Vanderschrick.

Point 6: Rue Vanderschrick

What makes this street special is not only is it an intact collection of Art Nouveau residential buildings, it has a string of 17 houses along the side of the street with the odd numbers designed by a single architect using Art Nouveau techniques to make each house different.

In the late 19th and early 20th Centuries, Brussels came to be known for the "Brussels House." The phenomenon resulted from a convergence of factors: A city rapidly expanding its footprint, an economy that enabled upper and middle classes to accumulate wealth, a customer base willing to invest their savings to build their own town houses, and a supply of young architects who emphasized craftsmanship and distinctive touches. As the work of these architects won favor, contractors and builders copied the style adding similar looking buildings, multiplying the impact. Brussels came to be known as an "Aesthetic City" and a leader in a movement known as "Applied Art in the Street."

The Brussels House featured a buried semi-level for a kitchen and cellar, a raised first floor with three rooms in a row, and two floors above for bedrooms, bathroom and study. It was common for a veranda on the first floor to overlook a walled garden invisible from the street. Topping the house was an attic that could be easily expanded. The Brussels House offered a much greater comfort level than other European houses at the time because of running water and toilets.

Rue Vanderschrick came about when a wealthy widow commissioned the architect Ernest Blerot to develop plans for the entire block of residences. Designing the block as a whole allowed Blerot to maintain the homogeneity of the houses and to schedule the work so as to reduce the time and cost of construction. This made the houses more affordable to the middle class which appealed to Blerot.

Construction was done in two stages. The eastern part of rue Vanderschrick (Nos. 1 to 13 and Nos. 13 and 15 at the corner with Waterloo) was built in 1900. The western part (Nos. 15 to 25 and Nos. 42 to 48 at the corner with Avenue Jean Volders) was built in 1902. The finished block was why Blerot became known as the "master of unity amid diversity." The facades have the same curved lines, the same template, arched windows and a cornice based on many corbels (supports extending from the wall).

There were, however, significant differences among the houses. A variety of construction materials were chosen. Some houses adopted white stone while the majority are adorned with light brick. Blerot located the bow windows at various levels and adorned the transoms of doorways or windows with a multitude of sgraffito. Yet, each house has at least one wrought iron balcony. Blerot himself designed the stained glass, sgraffito, ironwork, mosaics, woodwork and door handles. His signature adorns the entrances of his creations.

Among the features to look for as you walk down rue Vanderschrick:

- Waterloo 13, four sgraffito and a balcony with pair of windows.
- Corner of Waterloo and Vanderschrick, the oriel (a type of bay) window on two floors.
- Vanderschrick 3, the shop door.
- Vanderschrick 5, 7, 11, sgraffito floral patterns, with five having a curved ornament giving it the appearance of a piano.
- Vanderschrick 7, elevated doorway, balcony and bow window.
- Vanderschrick 9, entrance to a small park that you are welcome to visit by walking down an old mosaic path.
- Vanderschrick 19, bay windows and small timber ground floor.
- Vanderschrick 23 and 25, small windows with wood trim.
- Jean Volders 42/46, triangular stalls.

The real treat is at the end of the block at the intersection of Avenue Jean Volders. Blerot was also the architect for the building that now houses La Porteuse d'Eau, your Debriefing Point.

Point 7: La Porteuse d'Eau

Before entering take a step back from the front door, perhaps even crossing the street, to see the design of the roofline. The restaurant, rich in Art Nouveau design, is the perfect place to enjoy a beer, wine or tea, or a casual dinner or lunch. The bar offers a varied beer list and some selections can be paired with the appropriate cheese.

Ask for the special. Usual offerings include Troubadour Magma, a triple amber ale that combines a balanced Belgian ale with the hoppyness of an American IPA, and Poperings Hommel, a Belgian Golden pale ale with a strong hops flavor. Hommel is the Flemish word for hops. The café also may have Avec les Bons Voeux from Brasserie Dupont. The beer, brewed in the fall, began as a holiday

Walk 9 Map 2

gift for good clients of the brewery, a chance for it to send its "best wishes."

Point 8: Red Orchestra Safe House

When leaving the restaurant, turn right on Avenue Jean Volders, going down the hill.

A few doors away on the same side of the street, the former cobbler's shop at No. 32 is a point of interest because from 1938 to 1942 it was one of two safe houses for the Red Orchestra, an anti-Nazi, pro-Bolshevik organization. Founded in Germany in 1932, the group provided intelligence to the USSR about the Nazis and later offered resistance. In Belgium, the Red Orchestra gave ground reports via radio to the NKVD (forerunner of the KGB) and distributed anti-Nazi pamphlets. In December 1942, the group was disbanded with most of its members deported to Germany and executed in concentration camps.

As further evidence of the Saint Gilles neighborhood serving a nerve center of World War II resistance, the Mouvement National Belge

(MNB) had its headquarters on rue Vanderschrick next to la Porteuse d'Eau. The group assisted downed airmen under the motto "battus parfois – a battus Jamais" (sometimes beaten but never defeated).

Point 9: Porte de Halle

Continue walking down the hill to one of the city's ancient gates. Although much altered over the years, the castle-like building is now a museum whose artifacts describe the city's Medieval fortifications and life and which offers a panoramic view of the city. It also stakes claim to having the world's largest stuffed horse.

Porte de Halle dates from the 14th Century when it was part of the second set of walls that enclosed Brussels and its 50,000 inhabitants. The original gate included a draw bridge that allowed passage over a moat filled by local streams. Besides defense against invaders, the gate served as a watchtower for fires. Horns were blown by soldiers at the sign of a fire during a time when each house was required to have a pail from which water could be thrown to douse the flames.

No longer needed for defense, most of what remained of the Second Medieval Wall was torn down at the start of the 19th Century. Porte de Halle escaped destruction, however, because it had become a prison. You really did not want to be in prison during those times. Inmates were branded with markings for the prison's designation and their crime. Until the mid-19th Century, branding was done on the face.

No longer able to accommodate the growing city's prison population and running out of branding space, in the 1840s the tower became one of the city's first museums. Later, from 1868 to 1870, the tower was restored changing its Medieval appearance to a more romantic Neo-Gothic style and adding height with a conical roof encasing a giant stairway. A second renovation in the 2000s recreated the draw bridge. The side of the structure facing Saint-Gilles is truer to the original design than the side facing Brussels city center to the north.

One of the Tower's floors is the Guild Room where the story of Brussels' guilds is told. Guilds were not just for business relationships but were also an essential element of Middle Age urban life. Guilds provided like-minded people with opportunities to associate and to assist each other. Replicas of early 17th Century paintings of the Brussels Ommegang, or "walking around" in old Flemish, are displayed. The Ommegangs began as religious processions for relics or venerated images. By the 16th Century participation of the guilds was allowed by the Brussels' city elite in recognition of the guilds having helped to defend the city in the 15th Century. The butcher's guild was especially valuable in the city's defense and was a popular participant in the parade waving knives and skewers. Besides being able to join the procession, the guilds also earned a seat in city government to set policy regarding the protective walls.

Return: The Metro at Porte de Halle awaits your return at the bottom of Avenue Jean Volders.

Walk 10
Matonge and Ixelles

Africa Meets Europe

**Length of Walk: 1.5 hours
without museum or debrief
Museum Option: Museum of Ixelles**

Connecting Dots: The district now known in French as Ixelles and by its Flemish name Elsenat was first mentioned in history as Elsela, a name derived from a Dutch word meaning " alder woods," a family of trees that includes the birch. Located within the ancient forest stretching to the Medieval wall surrounding Brussels from southern Belgium, the first settlement outside the wall on the east was a 12th Century abbey. In the 16th Century castles appeared. Elsenat grew from hamlet to village. In 1795, the French occupiers of Brussels proclaimed Ixelles a separate municipality. From 1813 to 1900 the population of Ixelles increased from less than a thousand people to around 60,000 due its proximity to the recreational amenities and availability of land to build town-houses. The purity of water in the surrounding ponds attracted brewers. In 1860, a narrow band of land was annexed by the city of Brussels to build Avenue Louise, a transportation corridor to Boise de la Cambre, the former abbey turned into a park, further stimulating development. This resulted in the division of Ixelles into a section west of Avenue Louise and an eastern part that became home to the French-speaking Universitie Libre de Bruxelles and the Dutch-speaking Vrije Universiteit Brussels. Following the independence of the Congo in 1960 waves of Congolese students migrated to Brussels to study, settling in a section of Ixelles not far from

the Royal Palace and naming it Matonge. Today more than 100,000 African immigrants live in the area.

Starting Point: Metro at Port de Namur.

Point 1: Bastion Square

Stand at the entrance looking down Chaussee Ixelles. The square outside the Metro is the beginning of the road to the commune of Ixelles. It was created in1965 as part of an urban development plan.

The land that lay outside the wall of Brussels to the east was originally a wasteland called the Esplanade, a site used for military maneuvers. Following the dismantling of the fortifications surrounding Brussels in the late 18th Century, development began to take hold, first in the 1820s when the grand boulevard was built in place of the wall and in earnest in the 1850s, when the city annexed the Esplanade.

Point 2: Chausee d'Ixelles

The road exiting the fortification through the Esplanade led to the Belgian city of Namur. The convergence of two rivers in Namur made the city an important point on central Europe's east-west and north-south trade routes during Roman times. A Medieval castle that overlooked the rivers allowed whomever possessed it to control this strategic point along the routes. Unfortunately, this also meant the fortifications attracted invaders, including the Germans in both World Wars.

All the lands from the Medieval wall of Brussels to Namur were part of the Sonian Forest or Charcoal Forest. Covering virtually all southern Belgium, the forest produced the coal deposits of Wallonia that made it one of Europe's great industrial centers in the 18th and 19th Centuries.

Settlement in the area can be traced to the end of the 12th Century when a Benedictine nun founded the Abbey of La Cambre in the Maelbeek Valley within the forest about 4 kilometers (2.5 miles) from the Second Wall. A century later the Duke of Brabant built a hostel near the abbey to provide meals to the workers cutting trees in the forest.

Much of what had been built was destroyed during Medieval wars, but by the end of the 16th Century, stability allowed for the construction of small castles, country manors and chapels. The hamlet became a village. Being Belgium, brewers followed, drawn to the fresh water of the Maelbeek Valley ponds.

By the 1820s when city fortifications in eastern Brussels were demolished, the road to Namur was one of the important thoroughfares, serving both trade with lands to the east and the growing commune of Ixelles. The city erected toll gates in 1835 to collect taxes on goods entering Brussels at the intersection of the road to Namur and the new boulevard constructed where the wall had been. When the tax was abolished in 1860, the toll booths were relocated to the entrance of Boise de la Cambre as a park decoration.

With the population of the commune of Ixelles swelling in the last half of the 19th Century, Chaussee d'Ixelles as we see it today took shape. Street cars began serving Ixelles in 1894. The artists, professionals, merchants and industrialists who located here made it a center of Art Nouveau design when that style emerged at the end of the century.

Today, the intersection of Chaussee d'Ixelles and Boulevard du Regent marks the northern end of Brussels high-end shopping district. On its path to the east and the depths of the Maelbeek Valley, it serves as the main shopping district of Ixelles East.

Turn your back to Boulevard du Regent and the Metro entrance to walk along the left side of Chaussee d'Ixelles.

Point 3: Matonge

Walk past Chaussee de Wavre, a main avenue cutting off to the left. The second intersection past Chaussee de Wavre will be rue E. Solvay. Look for a sign on a post. There is no street sign in the usual location on the side of a building. Turn left.

You are in the Matonge, a section of Brussels that is the center of Brussels' 100,000 African immigrant community. A seemingly endless number of African hair dressing salons, barber shops, and small restaurants line the street.

Matonge takes its name from a section of Kinshasa, the capital city of the Democratic Republic of the Congo. After the Congo became independent of Belgium in 1960, a large of number of young Africans migrated to Brussels, encouraged by the establishment of La Maison Africaine, a hostel founded by the philanthropist Monique Van der Straten catering to African students. A Debriefing Point will be to your right at the first corner on E. Solvay.

Point 4: Ultimeatome

Ultimeatome is at the corner of E. Solvay and rue Saint Boniface, the street that runs directly away from the entrance of the church. There is a fine selection of beers and brasserie fare and a terrace from which to enjoy the street scene. Might as well try a wheat beer here. La Grande Blanche is often on draft. Poperings Hommel, a Belgian Golden Pale Ale from West Flanders, is a good bottle choice. Hommel is the Flemish word for hops.

If you want to return to the area for dinner and do not want to try the African food, Au Vieu Brussels is a traditional Belgian friterie serving moules and stews. It is one block further way from the church on rue Saint Boniface, on the other side of the street from Ultimeatome.

After the debrief, walk towards the church along rue Saint Boniface.

Point 5: Saint Boniface Church

Built in the Flemish church style, the church is the most outstanding feature of the Ixelles East landscape. Known for its stained-glass windows, the church is named after Saint Boniface, the bishop of Lausanne in the early 13th Century. Saint Boniface spent the last years of his life in the Abbey of La Cambre.

Turn left on rue de la Paix, the street in front of the church. Make the first right onto rue Longue Vie. A short way down on the right is Stam and a chance for a second debrief.

Point 6: Stam

Stam is taken from the old Brussels dialect meaning place to meet and drink. Ask for the draft of the month. A good standby is the Tripel Karmeliet.

Continue along rue Longue Vie heading away from Saint Boniface Church. Go one block and turn left on rue Anoul. When you reach Chaussee de Wavre, go right.

Grain d'Orge was a favored watering hole in the neighborhood at No. 142, but it recently closed. Perhaps you will be lucky and find it has reopened. If not, continue east along Chaussee de Wavre, going further away from Saint Boniface Church. Follow the road as it veers to the left. Beer Mania, just around the bend, offers a debrief and beer souvenir opportunity.

Point 7: Beer Mania

This is the store that supplies the US Embassy with its beers. Owner Nasser Eftekhari stocks over 400 Belgian Beers as well as an extensive range of beer-related products such as books and pre-packaged gift collections. More than 100 different types of Belgian Beer glasses can be found here. A tasting room in the back lets visitors enjoy the owner's own brand, Mea Culpa, a golden ale brewed with ten spices and served in Belgian crystal beer glasses of the owner's design.

With the debrief completed and your sack of beer merchandize in hand, backtrack to the bend at Chaussee de Wavre, and turn left, continuing east away from the church. A fine porcelain shop can be found at the intersection if you want a diversion from beer drinking.

Chausee de Wavre has become Rue Gopffart but you will not be on it long. At the first street, turn right onto rue du Conseil.

Walk four blocks through a residential neighborhood where you will find yourself again at Avenue Ixelles. At the corner on the right is your next visit, guess what, a debrief.

Point 8: Volle Gas

Legend has it a young man named Charles sat in the old café here writing to his lover, his Dear Maria, wondering if she would join him again at the house in the square that he had built for her. She had died a tragic death, a fall from a horse in Paris. Still he longed for her and imagined one day her vision would appear to him. "This old yellowed cardboard becomes the sole confidant of my impatience. Here, on the place clear-obscure, or the time seems to be arrested a slight breeze brings the scent of lilac hidden gardens. My heart panics: once more, in a shade close to the Hotel Communal, I thought I recognize your silhouette! Illusion!"

Charles is Belgian violinist Charles August de Beriot and his lover Maria Malibran, a famous opera singer who died in 1836 at age 28.

The square across from Volle Gaz was named for King Leopold when built in the early 19th Century. After it was enlarged later in the century, the square was renamed Ixelles Square. In 1920, it was renamed a final time to honor Fernand Cocq, an Ixelle mayor in the early 20th Century, defender of the French language and father of the painter Suzanne Cocq.

The stately building on the eastern side of the square is the manor that Charles August de Beriot built for Maria Malibran. For more than 100 years it has served as the Ixelles City Hall. The Neoclassical building's horizontal harmony remains intact despite renovations from 1905 to 1909.

Volle Gas was once the center for jazz in Brussels. The solid oak bar is assembled from 850 parts on the spot by a cabinetmaker taking 550 hours. How nice to imagine a Tongerlo Blonde from the draft sitting on the bar waiting for you. This blond Belgian ale has been voted best beer in world in recent years.

Leave Volle Gas and walk back along rue du Conseil. Make a right at rue Van Aa, the first intersection, continuing until it ends at No. 71 rue Jean Van Volsem.

Point 9: Museum of Ixelles

The Museum of Ixelles is known for its collection of 19th and 20th Century art, including impressionism, expressionism, fauvism, abstraction and surrealism. The museum is also known for frequent temporary exhibitions of modern art, photography and local history.

Ixelles is one of nineteen municipalities that comprise the Brussels Region of Belgium. The word is a derivation of Else, meaning "alder woods." Alder is the tree family to which birch belong.

In 1795, the ruling French regime proclaimed Ixelles independent. In 1813, the city only had 677 residents. But in the years following the removal of the fortifications surrounding Brussels and with the emergence of trams and street cars, the population swelled. By 1900, the population had grown to 58,000, including artists, celebrities and businessmen who hired architects to design

distinctive townhomes. Living outside city center with green space yet with all the modern conveniences was all the rage at the turn of the 20th Century.

When you leave the museum, turn to your right along Jean Van Volsem and make an immediate right onto rue Sans Souci. After one block, make another right onto rue Malibran. Pass several intersections. A big open market and transportation hub will be on your left. Keep walking to the corner of Chaussée d'Ixelles.

Point 10: Place Flagey

The large open area is Place Flagey built on land that was until 1860 at the bottom of a pond.

Named in honor of Eugene Flagey, Ixelles mayor from 1935 to 1953, the square has long been a transportation hub, with ten streets flowing into it. The Art Deco building on the eastern end of the square is the former Maison de la Radio, the radio broadcast center for Belgium. Its design was meant to resemble a steam ship, a reoccurring theme in Art Deco architecture, so much so that the style is often referred to as "steam ship."

In 2002 the building was renamed "Flagey," and it became the home of the Brussels Philharmonic and recording studios. Across the square is the Delhaize grocery, which opened in 1957 as the first supermarket in Belgium, and Frit Flagey, one of the city's best known friteries.

More significantly for this book, the Flagey building is the home of Cafe Belga.

Point 11: Cafe Belga

You have earned a well-deserved beer. Cafe Belga is on the ground floor of the Flagey building. The wrap around terrace of the Art Deco bar is a favorite spot to enjoy a beer.

There are many good beer choices here, including ones from American craft breweries like Ommegang. But this book is about Belgian beers not American. Try a Duvel Triple Hop Golden Ale. Duvels are easy to drink, known as "iron fists in golden gloves."

Point 12: Ixelles Ponds

The recommended plan is to sit on the terrace of the Café Belga and look out on the two fresh water ponds adjacent to Place Flagey.

In ancient times, many such ponds dotted the Valley of the Maelbeek. In the 1700s and 1800s the water in the streams and ponds was so noted for its freshness and purity that breweries located here, several surviving until the 20th Century. Beer was such an important part of the Brussels economy that the authorities abolished duties on the production and consumption of beer, encouraging farmers to switch from cultivation of wheat and beans to barely and hops.

Most ponds were drained at the end of the 19th Century to gain land for development as was done to create what is now Place Flagey. Today, the water in these two surviving ponds is so heavily polluted that even though ducks and geese call the ponds home, humans are warned against sitting on the grass near the water's edge.

Point 13: Eglise Sainte Croix

In the back and to the right of the Flagey building is Holy Cross Church. It began its existence a short distance away as a chapel dating from 1300 when it served as a resting place for the gatherers of wood returning to Ixelles from the Soignes forest. The chapel provided a horse to help the workers with their transport. In 1802, the chapel, which had been rebuilt several times over the years, was recognized as a parish church.

In 1856 as part of the work to fill in some of the ponds located here, a royal decree was issued to rebuild the church on reclaimed land at the northern tip of the pond. Because of the spongy nature of the soil, however, the church was not placed in the center of the square but at the location where it stands today. Originally designed in a Gothic Revival style by the architect Van de Wiele and built in red brick and white stone, it was rebuilt between 1940 and 1942 by the engineer-architect Paul Rome when Art Deco characteristics were added.

Point 14: General de Gaulle Avenue

Cross the avenue bordering Place Sainte Croix and go past the monument honoring Charles de Coster at the end of the pond. De Coster was a 19th Century Belgian literary figure who mastered 16th Century French because he claimed his native Flemish manners and speech could not be faithfully composed in modern French. The monument shows the heroes of his masterpiece "The Legend of Thyl Ulenspiegel and Lamme Goedzak." On the sides of the monument are various elements that evoke traditional interiors of a Flemish house: a rack, a spinning wheel, a distaff, a cat and a dog. De Coster died in 1879 and is buried in Ixelles.

Turn left to walk along General de Gaulle Avenue on the right side of the pond. You will only walk one block, to the small roundabout. You can sit on a bench to rest as you learn more about the buildings along the avenue.

Ratified by royal decree in 1873, the avenue replaced an old trail on property owned by the Abbey de la Cambre that dated from the 13th Century. Timber merchants and peasants used the trail when gathering wood and brush. The trail became so heavily used that in 1581 the Abbey was allowed to install barriers to control access. In 1876 when the construction of the ponds was completed, the trail was named "avenue of the waterfall" referring to an artificial breakwater located at the end of the big pond. The avenue was renamed in honor of the French General Charles de Gaulle in 1945.

The first buildings along the avenue were permitted in the late 1870s, but most of the construction occurred between the late 1880s to early 1900s. To preserve the tranquility of the ponds as a recreational area, the commune of Ixelles required that homes have an easement of eight meters in front of each facade to allow the development of garden landscape designs.

Eclecticism was in vogue when the first houses were constructed. Nos. 30, 31 and 33 by Ernest Delune reflect this. At No. 44, the Liège architect Paul Jaspar designed a picturesque Mosan façade, a Romanesque style of art originating in the Meuse valley in Central Europe in the 11th Century. Houses at Nos. 38 and 39 are by the architect Ernest Blérot, known as the "master of unity amid diversity." He built more than 60 houses in the communes of Ixelles and Saint-Gilles, including his own house that stood on the corner of the avenue and rue Vilain XIV at the far end of the big pond. It was demolished in the early 1960s.

Beginning at the end of the 1930s, a few private houses along the avenue were replaced by modernist apartment buildings, a trend that became popular in post-World War I Brussels. No. 25-26 is by the modernist architect Jacques Saintenoy at the corner of the rue Lannoy. The Streamline Moderne "Barrel" at No 51 evokes the curves of the ponds in a style where Art Deco is stripped of its ornament in favor of the aerodynamic pure-line concept of motion and speed, emphasizing curving forms, long horizontal lines, and sometimes nautical elements. The "Cascade" or "Waterfall" built in 1938-1939 by architect Rene Ajoux is at No. 36. In promoting his works Ajoux wrote to his clients, "The pursuit of beautiful, sustainable, architectural and decorative art will always be my only goal. The softness in shape, comfort and harmony of color are always the most important elements."

Time to rejoin the walk to the last destination. Turn right at the roundabout near the midway point of the big pond, taking the second street rue de la Vallee. At the fork bear right up on the hill onto rue de Lac.

Point 15: House of the Glass Craftsman

At rue du Lac 6 is one of the iconic images of Art Nouveau design. It was designed by Ernest Delune in 1902 to be the studio and home of Austrian master glass maker Clas Grüner Sterner. Sterner made the windows in his house as well as for several neighbors. Floral patterns decorate the windows with the circular doorway and large bow window, the house's most distinctive features. The window traces the stairwell inside.

Return: Walk along the pond to the transportation hub at Flagey. Hop on the 81 Tram direction Marius Renard. At the second stop, Bailli, exit. Now on Avenue Louise, you can transfer to the 93 or 94 Trams to return to the Metro at Louise.

Walk 11
The Marolles

Scavenger Hunt with a Local Flavor

Length of Tour: 1 hour without debrief

Connecting Dots: During the Middle Ages, small clusters of people lived within the ancient walls of Brussels to the south. Among them was a house for lepers. Beginning around the 18th Century, the area and its inhabitants came to be known as Les Marolles, a reference to an order of nuns who lived in the area in the 17th Century. During the French revolutionary occupation at the end of the 18th Century, the leper house became a hospital where the city of Brussels would later concentrate its medical infrastructures. Another transformation was the construction of small homes and shops for the workers employed in the city's small industries. In the 19th Century the Marolles was impacted by construction of the Palace of Justice on the high ground where public hangings once took place. Today, new immigrants to Brussels live in many of the small homes once occupied by the factory workers. In a parallel evolution, furniture and antique stores and trendy cafes have moved into the spaces of long-time merchants. But the Brussels dialect of Flemish still can be heard among the natives living here, and the open-air flea market held every morning evokes Medieval commerce.

Starting Point: Entrance to Metro at Louise.

Point 1: Avenue Louise

Avenue Louise begins here heading east. Commissioned in 1847 as a grand transportation corridor

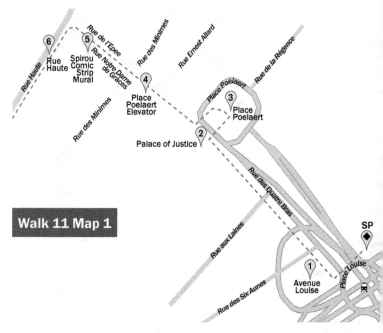

Walk 11 Map 1

to take city dwellers to the picnic grounds of Bois de la Cambre, today it is Brussels' high end shopping district.

The focus of this tour, however, is not the chestnut tree-lined avenue but the Marolles, the southern section of Brussels' Lower Town. Standing at Louise Metro, turn to the west and walk towards the gold domed building encased in scaffolding, the Palace of Justice.

Point 2: Palace of Justice

The Palace of Justice, the Belgium Supreme Court, dominates the Upper Town's skyline. It sure provides for a lot of justice, some 26,000 square meters (almost 280,000 square feet) of it.

Built by Leopold II as part of his master plan to transform Brussels into a major European metropolis, the building caused the demotion of 3,000 houses stretching into the Marolles neighborhood below when its construction began in 1863. Not only were the displaced families upset from having a forced relocation to the outskirts of the city, the local populace in general was outraged when it was learned the city gave healthy reimbursements to landlords. The project was so disliked, the word architect itself became an insult. Much to popular delight at the time, the project's architect Joseph Poelaert is said to have gone mad from the massive structure's symmetrical demands. He died four years before the building's inauguration in 1883.

The Palace of Justice stands as the largest building built in Europe during the 19th Century. It is also considered the antithesis of the Art Nouveau movement which soon followed. While the frame of the Palace of Justice is made of steel, it is covered in stone making it still today the largest stone structure in Europe.

Don't let the scaffolding fool you. The building is open to the public and is where civil legal cases are decided. In the 1980s when stones started falling from the façade, the city surrounded the upper floors in scaffolding. In 2003 the reguilded dome was revealed and some scaffolding removed. In 2010, with the renovation at a standstill, the city bought scaffolding to hold up the scaffolding. The firm that installed the original scaffolding had gone bankrupt. In 2012, scaffolding was added to block off the entrance and the bronze door that was erected in 1896.

You get the idea. The building is falling apart. Current plans are to re-initiate the renovation with a targeted completion date of 2028. Most view that as optimistic. Meanwhile the building is a monument to scaffolding as much as justice.

Go inside during working hours to see the waiting room's symmetrical details and statues of Demosthenes and Cicero. Lawyers meet with their clients at tables in the grand hall before seeing a magistrate. If you venture into the basement records' chambers, wear a mask to protect yourself against mold.

Point 3: Place Poelaert

Outside the Palace of Justice is Place Poelaert, one of the largest squares in Brussels. It was built from 1867 to 1883. The panoramic view stretches from the Lower Town to the symbol of the Brussels World's Fair of 1958, the Atonium. The Atonium features nine stainless steel spheres forming the shape of an iron crystal, a nod to one of the industries that propelled the Belgian economy to the forefront of the Continent's industrial revolution.

Place Poelaert, named after palace's architect, sits on Galgenberg or Mount of Strength. Long before construction of the Palace of

Justice, the city administered justice here by holding public hangings. Today, Galgenberg hosts a memorial dedicated to World War I soldiers. The Belgian Law Courts, also designed by Poelaert, sit across from the Palace of Justice.

Point 4: Place Poelaert Elevator

On the left side of the viewing terrace is the entrance to the Place Poelaert Elevator. Take it to the heart of the Marolles.

The free ride takes only 30 seconds. The lift is extremely weight sensitive and if too full will not move. One by one passengers will have to exit until the doors close.

Below is Place Breughel, named in honor of the Flemish painter Pieter Breughel, the Elder, who lived in Brussels in the 16th Century. A member of a family of painters, Pieter was known as the "Peasant Buegel."

Point 5: Spirou Comic Strip Mural

Walk away from the elevator. A comic strip mural will be on the side of a building to your left. The protagonist of the strip, Spirou, or mischievous one, is surrounded by dealers of second-hand goods. Originally an elevator operator at the fictional Moustique Hotel, Spirou later becomes a magazine reporter fighting villains all over the world even though he continues to wear the red uniform from his elevator days.

More than 50 murals of famous comic strip scenes created by Belgian artists can be found throughout the city. The Marolles is especially rich in them. The websites of the Visit Brussels Tourist Center and the Belgian Comic Strip Center have maps to locate them. More on the relevance of the mural's placement in the Marolles later in the walk.

Walk to rue Haute, the street at the bottom of Place Brueghel. Turn left.

Point 6: Rue Haute

Stretching out more than a kilometer (nearly 0.7 miles), rue Haute is the longest street within Brussels' inner ring. It is also one of the city's oldest, dating to the Roman era. Rue Haute runs the length of the Marolles, a district whose name is believed to have derived from the 17th Century nuns who settled in the area to be close to the city's poor. As they were famous for being Mariam colentes (those who honor the Virgin Mary), the nuns became known as 'Maricolles', which was later contracted to 'Marolles.'

Despite being a poor neighborhood, the Marolles has always been a lively one, at one time full of bars, dance halls and cinemas. Today, the cinemas, dance halls and old bars are gone. In their place are numerous antique, vintage and second-hand shops, as well as new restaurants and watering holes.

The Marolles still has hints of Brussels' Medieval residents. Those native to the area speak the Brussels dialect of Flemish. Their forebears lived for generations in the tiny houses that line the streets running off the avenues like rue Haute, serving as the workforce for the small factories that were concentrated in the Lower Town near the river from the 17th Century to the 20th Century. But the area is definitely in transition. Residents fear the uniqueness that is the Marolles will be lost and the area will become an extension of its northeast neighbor the Sablon, famous for its exclusive antique shops, high-end restaurants, trendy bars, expensive apartments – and being Brussels, chocolate shops.

Take in the string of bric-brac, furniture and small antique shops along rue Haute and the side streets. The third street that enters from the right is rue des Renards. Walk one more block, to the fourth street entering from the right, rue de la Rasiere (the street sign will be on your right). Look down the street to find rows of orange colored brick buildings.

Point 7: Cite Hellemans

Cite Hellemans sits on the left side of rue de la Reasiere.

The complex, designed in the Art Nouveau style by Emile Hellemans, opened in 1915 as Brussels first large scale public housing project and one of Europe's earliest experiments in social housing. Cite Hellemans introduced a new type of residential structure aimed at reducing the unhealthy living conditions that plagued working class neighborhoods.

By 1800, the area south of the Grand Place had become a maze of winding streets twisting over and around old farmland and the gardens of town homes, a consequence of rapid growth and the needs of small factories in need of an unskilled workforce. At mid-century with Brussels the capital of a new European nation and a prosperous one at that, the city government cleared land to build avenues that would support commerce and further growth.

The first was rue Blaes built from 1853 to 1858 parallel to the old north-south route of rue Haute. Traffic flow was improved. Police and fire brigades could more easily move through the area. Substandard housing was destroyed. But no solution was offered to provide nearby housing for the families of laborers who were displaced. The traditional approach was to move them to the outskirts of the city, away from their jobs.

By the turn of the 20th Century, city leaders in Brussels, like in other European cities, concluded that government must engage in housing as part of urban renewal projects to permanently stem the creation of slums which were breeding grounds for revolutionary thought and mass protest.

Planning for what became known as Cite Hellemans began in 1903. A dozen dead-end streets were located here, inhabited by several thousand people living in squalid conditions with rampant crime.

Cite Hellemans was a radical departure from traditional thought. Hellemans' plan was to create shared living conditions in a series of parallel blocks, offering an alternative to destroying neighborhoods and replacing them with housing for more affluent classes. The concept was to introduce a new type of housing in areas that had become slums that did not require excluding the poor.

Construction of the 272 units in Cite Hellemans took place between 1912 and 1915. Wide walkways connected by passages under arcades provided for air flow and for sunlight to fill spaces between buildings and inside apartments. Designing the arched passages to intersect perpendicularly connected the seven buildings visually. Giving them names like street of chimney sweeps and street of coopers (or chair makers) dignified the work of the laborers who lived in the Marolles. Following the Art Nouveau style, Hellemans used bands of polychrome brick to unify the buildings as a single creation while wrought iron and stone features on the exterior distinguished them.

Apartments were limited to two per floor, discouraging gathering in stairways. The apartments shared a common kitchen and dining area, but each had three bedrooms: one for parents, one for boys and one for girls. Each apartment also had a south-facing terrace for relaxation and everyday household work such as laundry. Use of the terraces to hang laundry enabled the open courtyards between buildings to be free of clutter and congestion. Running water in the apartments provided living conditions superior to those for residents in many other areas of Brussels.

Cite Hellemans is still in use as public housing. Families that recently immigrated to Brussels live in the units, hanging their laundry on the south facing terraces as did the residents before them.

Return to rue Haute and retrace your steps one block to rue des Renards.

Point 8: Escargot Push Cart

A special treat in the Marolles is a stop at a push cart serving escargot. At one time, they were common in the city's working class neighborhoods, offering a quick meal and chance to trade local news and gossip. A single family has operated a cart located at one end or the other of rue des Renards for generations. The snails are well cooked and quite safe to eat, but remember to spit out the feet.

Turn down the hill at rue des Renards.

Point 9: Restobieres

Debriefing Points usually occur at the end of each walk. This walk is no exception. But a place along this street offers too much appeal to pass up.

Restobieres is on the left. In Brussels, unlike a café, you cannot simply go into a restaurant to order a beer without a meal. Restobieres is a restaurant, but one every beer drinker will want to visit. If it is not time for lunch or dinner as you pass by, stop inside to reserve for later.

Most of the dishes are cooked with beer. The roasted Chimay cheese as a starter is a house specialty. Restobieres offers excellent beer list, including several lambics and bottles branded for the owner, Alain Fayt. It is the perfect place to have a lunch or dinner either during or after your walk. A recommended beer choice is the Hercules Stout, named after the famed Belgian detective Hercule Poirot and said to be the only true Belgian made stout. If you would like a blonde ale, try the Lupulus a bieres ou fut (on draft) from the Ardennes with an alcohol proof of 8.5%. A third choice is the Cuvee de Ranke, a Belgian pale ale that is a fresh sour beer like kriek but without the cherries. It is fun to unwrap the blue wrapper that decorates the bottle.

After passing second hand dress shops, you arrive at rue Blaes. The cafe Brocanti is on the corner. The name translates to "where people sell their old stuff." You will learn the significance of the translation at the next stop. If you decide to stop here for a beer, there is a good list of gueze beers: The very expensive Horal's Grand Gueze Mega Blend; Tilquin Gueze; 3 Fonteinen; and Boon Gueze Mariage Parfeit among them. Another spontaneous fermentation choice if in stock is Cantillon Iris. Unlike most lambics that use 100% dried hops, Iris uses 50%. The marsh iris is the flower of Brussels having grown abundantly in the marsh land that predated Grand Place and the area around the River Senne. A gueze beer also goes well as an aperitif before one of the dishes at Restobieres.

Head diagonally across rue Blaes to Place du Jeu de Balle. If you have arrived in the morning or early afternoon, a flea market is in full swing.

Point 10: Place du Jeu de Balle

Les Marolles occupies the southern part of the Pentagon that is at the heart of Brussels, and Place du Jeu de Balle lies at the center of Les Marolles life. Walk down the right side of the square unless you want to take a stroll through the merchants and return here.

Remember Spirou, the former elevator operator? The mural you saw depicted him here.

In the Middle Ages, two markets operated within the southern arc of Brussels' wall. In those ancient times, trade was often subdivided into "new sale" and "second-hand sale."

In the 17th Century, a new square intended for the "second-hand sale" market of rags and old clothes was fitted out on the left bank of the river Senne at Place Anneessens. With the development of the central boulevards to transform the city, the "second-hand sale" market needed to move again. In 1873, the city moved it into Les Marolles, giving it the name of the "new old market."

Place du Jeu de Balle's history dates to before the market's relocation. From 1839 until 1844, a factory which produced locomotives was active here. The factory, named Renard (Fox in English), later served as a workshop for the painter Antoine Wiertz.

In 1858 a square was fitted out in the middle of the new rue Blaes in the place of the former factory. It was named 'Vossenplein' in Dutch and 'Place du Jeu de Balle' in French, referring to the sport 'jeu de balle' (handball). It was a natural choice for the "new old market" and is the only open air market in Brussels that operates every day.

Residents shop for clothes and furnishings. Mixed in with the everyday necessities is an occasional antique. There is also a lot of junk. When the market closes, some merchants simply leave items behind, either for scavengers or for the city's trash collectors.

Point 11: Baines de Bruxelles

Just past where the square ends, another vestige of the past still operates. It is located on the street to the right of square that you have been walking down.

Bains de Bruxelles at 28 rue du Chevreuil is probably the most impressive public swimming pool in Belgium. Built in 1949, this modernist building allows swimmers views of the city from the pool on the 3rd floor.

Walk back up to rue Blaes.

Point 12: Rue Blaes

Start your return to city center by walking along rue Blaes, turning left. Like Rue Haute, Rue Blaes has shop after shop of furniture, bric-a-brac, art, vintage clothing and collectibles.

In 1942, Belgium began to experience oppression from its German occupiers. In the east, Jews were forced into labor. Large round-ups occurred in Antwerp and Liege with the assistance of local police. In Brussels, Mayor Jules Coelst told the Germans he was sorry but the police could not help. Earlier, he had refused to distribute the occupier's yellow star to the city's Jewish population.

Yet, on September 3 at about 8:30 PM, the Marolles area was sealed off. Two Brussels police officers closed off the streets, and the German occupiers searched houses. Foreign Jews of all ages and sexes were pushed into trucks that drove them to barracks in Mechelen, between Brussels and Antwerp. It was the first step in deportation to Auschwitz for the 718 Jews arrested that day.

Point 13: Comic Strip Murals on rue des Capucins

The first intersection is rue des Capucins. Look to the left.

On the side of a building at the far end of the street is a scene from "Blondin & Cirage," a strip by the Belgian artist Franquin Jije. The series tells the adventures of a white boy named Blondin and a black boy named Shine. The series debuted in 1939 as a new way of educating Belgian children. Here we meet Marsupilami, an imaginary animal invented by Jijé to be a companion on the boys' time adventures.

Go further down the street and you will find one more mural at your back, a creation of Turk and de Groot. Here, the main character Leonard, inspired by Leonardo da Vinci, lives in the early Renaissance period. The strip, however, includes aspects of 20th Century life. In this scene Leonard is flanked by Basile, his long-suffering and reluctant assistant. Léonard refers to his younger helper as "Disciple" ("Lackey" in the English version), while Basile calls him "Master". Raul the cat also is in the scene.

Return to rue Blaes, continuing to the left until it terminates (along with rue Haute) at Place de la Chappelle.

An interesting point along the way is No. 184, an impasse that hosted "Maison de Toone," the Brussels puppet theater now near Grand Place. It was here at Impasse de Varsovie, under the direction of Toone V, that the troop conducted a "pornographic" puppet performance with a naked Woltje having his way with a "toffe mokske," a nice girl. The 1930s audience shouted "Curtain!" forcing the theater to temporarily close. The end of the theater off rue Blaes came during a November night in 1944 when the only V-bomb to fell on Brussels landed a few steps from the theater, destroying seventy-five puppets. Toon VI now running the theater gathered the survivors puppets and stored them in an old stable

On the left further along rue Blaes is a comic strip mural between Nos. 121 and 119. Benoit Brisefer is a little man with a big heart and herculean strength that he loses if he catches a cold. He lives in a village that looks like the Marolles. Known for his kindness and spontaneity, the mural captures him at his best, taking a giant leap to catch an escaping balloon.

Point 14: Eglise Notre-Dame de le Chappelle

The church at Place de la Chappelle, rebuilt in the early 15th Century in the Romanesque and Romanesque-Gothic style, sits on the site of a chapel dating from 1134 that served craftsmen living just outside the first Brussels wall. In 1250 the church received

Walk 11 Map 3

what was claimed to be five pieces from the cross of the Crucifixion making it a Medieval pilgrimage site.

One of the chapels preserves the memory of Pieter Bruegel the elder, who was buried in the church in 1569. Also inside the church, a plaque commemorates Francois Annessens, a leader in the Brussels guilds who was executed by the city's Austrian rulers in 1719. At the end of the War of Spanish Succession, the lands including Belgium were awarded to the Austrians. They quickly raised taxes and challenged the Medieval guilds who effectively ran the city. Riots resulted which were brutally suppressed. Annessens was lured to attend a meeting with an Austrian colonel who then arrested him and kept him captive along with three other guild leaders. After six months, Annessens was condemned to death. The three others were sentenced to permanent exile.

Walk along the side of the church following rue de la Chapelle. Skate Park Place De La Chapelle will be on your left. Turn to the right, then making the second left onto rue des Alexiens.

Point 15: Porte Noire or La Fleur en Papier Doré

Porte Noire is a vaulted tavern at No. 67, the converted kitchen of a 17th Century convent. Be warned the tavern usually does not open until 5 PM and usually not all on Sundays. A dozen or so beers are on draft. One frequent draft resident is Brusseleir, a dark IPA distinguished by its rich malt character and light chocolate notes at 8% from Brasserie de la Senne. Another is VanderGhinste Oud Bruin, a light stout cut with lambic that is a typical West Flanders red beer. A third is the Cuvée Ranke, a fruity mix between a lambic and a blond. If you would like a lighter beer, look for a Barbar Golden Honey Ale.

La Fleur en Papier Doré at rue des Alexiens 53/5 offers a bonus besides good sausage and beer. On the summer terrace is a comic strip mural of Stam & Pilou. It joins the photographs of the Belgian surrealists like René Magritte, Louis Scutenaire, Marcel Mariën who used to dine – and drink – here. Stam, the boy, is not as good an acrobat as he thinks. Pilou, the girl-next-door, sits on his head while Grandpa Fons studies Stam's mother's rear end. Grandpa is a retired postman and an avid stamp collector. The strip was produced at the request of the Belgian Post Office and appeared in the magazine of a stamp club for young people. The board that Grandpa holds has the words "Sprekt a mooiertoêl, ARA!" which is Brussels dialect for "speak your mother tongue." ARA is an organization that supports the Brussels dialect. For a touch of irony, order a La Trappe Quadrupel. It is brewed in the Netherlands but is a good one nonetheless.

Return: Walk back to rue de la Chapelle which will become Boulevard de l'Empereur and turn left. Walk until you reach Brussels Central and the Metro there. Alternatively, you can walk down rue des Alexiens to the Annessens underground tram station to return to the center city.

Walk 12
Anderlecht

Beer and Chocolates

**Length of Walk: 1.5 hours
without museums and debriefs
Museum Options: Brewers Museum •
Chocolate Museum • Cantillon Brewery**

Connecting Dots: Brewing beer dates to when humans began growing crops. Around 4000 BC the Sumerians in Mesopotamia used a barley mixture to produce an early version of beer. By 3000 BC the Egyptians were flavoring beer with spices. The modern age of beer brewing began in the Middle Ages when monks added hops to fermented barley to balance its flavor. This better enabled the church to capitalize on market demand created by the lack of sanitary drinking water. Commercial interests followed. In the Senne River Valley, an area favorable to brewing because of the wild yeasts found there, enterprising merchants formed the first brewer's guild. In the late 19th Century technological innovations revolutionized brewing. Louis Pasteur identified yeast strains most suitable for making beer. Availability of electricity for industrial purposes and the invention of industrial refrigeration enabled beer to be made from yeast fermenting at low temperatures, creating pils beer. New filtering technologies improved the quality of beer, and techniques for glass production and introduction of rail transport enabled producers to serve expanded markets. In Belgium, the old brewing styles survived as newer techniques came to dominate world markets. Traditional brewing is part of Belgium's culture.

Starting Point: Grand Place. Head to the Brewers Guild, the building topped by the equestrian statue.

Point 1: Museum of Belgian Brewers

The basement of the Brewers Guild houses a museum dedicated to the history of beer, including equipment from a traditional 18th Century brewery. Check on the hours. The museum normally opens at 10 AM Monday to Friday and noon Saturday and Sunday.

The house itself was built in the 14th Century and named Gulden Den Boom or Golden Tree. The Brewers Guild, which was also founded in the 14th Century, bought the house in the 16th Century. After the French Bombardment of 1695 destroyed it and much everything else in Grand Place, the brewers began its reconstruction, adding Baroque and Flemish decorative styles evident today. The gold leafed equestrian statue added in 1901 depicts Charles of Lorraine, the guild's benefactor.

There is not one type of beer that is Belgian. Many types of beers are brewed in the country:

- Ales (Amber, Blond, Brown, Scotch, Dubble, Tripel, and Champagne)
- Flemish Red and Flemish Sour Brown
- Hop Accentuated Beers
- Pils
- Saison
- Stout
- Wheat Beer
- Christmas or Winter Beers
- And the most unique, the Lambic beers (including Gueuze and Fruit Beers).

Trappist and Abbey beers are not types of beers but certifications stating who the brewer is. Their tastes and styles vary greatly.

Also, there is no one fermentation style. Typically, beers with greater alcoholic content like ales, porters and stouts are top fermentation beers. Yeast cells are carried to the top of the fermenting liquid at a

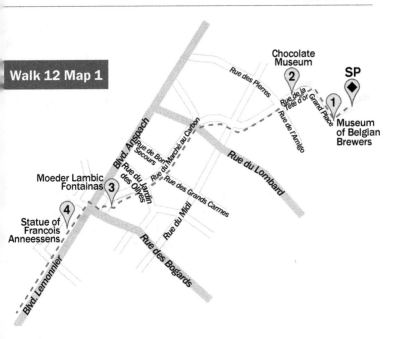

Walk 12 Map 1

higher temperature than is used for bottom fermentation beers. Pils is an example of a bottom fermentation beer. Yeasts are brewed at lower temperatures, grow less rapidly and produce less foam.

Lambic beers are produced from spontaneous fermentation. That style is unique to Belgium, and we will learn about it at Cantillon Brewery, a few steps (and beers) away.

What is characteristic of Belgian beer, no matter what the type, is the use of yeast to create the beer's flavor. Different yeast strains produce different flavors and balance the other contributors to a beer's flavor: hop, malt and spices.

Enjoy the tour and the tasting in the small cafe at the Brewers Guild.

After exiting the guild building, turn left in Grand Place, passing in front of the City Hall and exiting the square at rue de la Tête d'or at the southwest corner.

Point 2: Chocolate Museum

Just off Grand Place at No. 9 is Le Musée du Cacao et du Chocolat. A chocolatier demonstrates how melted chocolate is shaped into pralines, providing samples along the way. Displays tell the story of how cocoa beans are collected in Africa and turned into chocolate. A section describes how chocolate has been consumed in Europe throughout the centuries.

You must not visit Brussels without sampling its chocolate. At least one shop and usually more – whether it be one of the famous brands such as Leonidas, Godiva, Neuhaus or Marcolini or a shop operated by an artisan chocolatier – can be found on every walk in this book.

The history of chocolate begins 4000 years ago when the Aztec and Mayan cultures cultivated the cocoa tree in the tropical plains of South America. Cocoa was so important to these ancient peoples that the beans were used as a currency to barter, pay taxes and buy slaves.

The Mayas were the first to produce a drink from the cocoa bean, flavoring it with peppers and incorporating it into religious ceremonies where chocolate was associated with Xochiquetzal, their goddess of fertility.

Before the 16th Century, nobody in Europe had heard about the popular chocolate drink consumed in South and Central America. That changed in July 1502 when Christopher Columbus "discovered" chocolate on Guanaja, one of the bay islands of Honduras. The importation of chocolate in Europe began a few decades later when the Spanish conquered the Aztecs and introduced the drink to Spain and its colonies soon making it the preferred beverage of high society rather than tea or coffee. The Spanish early on sweetened it with sugar cane.

In 1657 chocolate began to be more affordable when the first chocolate factory opened in London and Hans Sloane developed a milk chocolate drink. During the industrial revolution in the 1700s, hard chocolates made their appearance.

On a street one block from the opposite corner of Grand Place, Chocopolis at 110 rue du Marche aux Herbes has a fine selection of chocolates, all made on the premises and visible to visitors.

For the next stop, continue along rue de la Tête d'or walking away from Grand Place. The street becomes rue du Marche au Charbon.

Follow it until it ends at Place Fontainas and Boulevard Maurice Lemonnier. No. 8 Pace Fontainas is the next visit.

Point 3: Moeder Lambic Fontainas

Moeder Lambic (Lambic Mother) offers a unique beer experience. A sister bar is on the Art Nouveau walk.

While beer types like pils, stouts and ales are brewed either at low or high temperatures with cultivated strains of yeasts, lambics are produced by spontaneous fermentation using wild yeasts and air born bacteria found only in Belgium. For the lambics, brewers use aged, dry hops that have lost their bitterness. After the fermentation process starts, lambics are siphoned off into wine or sherry barrels where they mature for one, two or three years.

At Moeder Lambic you can usually taste all the types of lambic beers: Gueuze (a mixture of young lambics), faro (a sweetened lambic), kriek (refermented with cherries), and fruit lambic (with other fruits added as syrups or in their entirety). Several of the lambics are hand pumped from casks allowing the beer to be served in its natural state. Snack on the barley seeds as you sip.

Often Lindemans Faro beer is available as is the Gueuzerie Tilquin gueuze beer from the Senne valley, said to be the only gueuze blendery in Wallonia, the French speaking part of Belgium.

It is time to see how lambic beer is brewed.

Exit Moeder Lambic, cross Boulevard Maurice Lemonnier (the southern section of Boulevard Anspach), and turn left. Enjoy a stroll along the boulevard although it has lost its luster when compared to how it appeared at the turn of the 20th Century.

Point 4: Statue of Francois Anneessens

On the right is a statue of one of Brussels leading citizens. He was so prominent, he had the honor of being decapitated in Grand Place in 1719. A craftsman who was a leader in the slate cutting and chair making guilds, Francois Anneessens fought for the rights of craft guilds to expand their political power in the city, leading the movement to resist new taxes imposed by the Austrian rulers. Popular opinion was with guilds. Rioting ensured. Only the arrival of Austrian troops restored peace. Again in power, the Austrians ordered the execution of Anneessens and banished leaders of four other guilds.

To the rear of the statue is the Institute Lucien Cooremans, a former elementary school named in honor of a Brussels mayor. The side facing the boulevard is designed in the Flemish Renaissance style to convey prosperity and communal power. The entrance porch recreates 16th and 17th Century Flemish palace style.

The statue and school reside in what is now called Anneessens Square. Until vaulting of the Senne, the site hosted the "old market" for second hand clothes and rags. The desire to attract affluent residents who would live and shop along the prestigious new boulevards caused the city to relocate the market into the Marolles, where the "new old market" now resides. In 1889 the gentrified square was named in honor of Anneessens.

Continue along Boulevard M. Lemonnier.

Point 5: Palais du Midi

It is not worth a stop, but it is so big, you are likely looking at the building on your left. Palais du Midi was built between 1875 and 1880 by the General Company of Markets. Today, the markets have been for the most part replaced by indoor sports activities. It must have really been something special in its day.

Cross Boulevard du Midi at where Boulevard M. Lemonnier ends.

Point 6: Midi Station

After crossing Boulevard du Midi, you can see the elevated train tracks that lead to Midi train station. The station serves the fast trains serving London, Paris and other European cities.

Several generations of train stations served the southern end of the city before the current building was constructed in the 20th Century as part of the north-south rail connection that runs through the city. Each station was bigger than the one before.

Directly outside the station is Tour du Midi or South Tower, a 38-story skyscraper constructed in the 1960s. It is the tallest building in Belgium and when constructed was the tallest building in the European Union. The Belgian Pensions Administration occupies it.

Walk 12 Map 2

If you are lucky to visit in July or August, the Midi Fair is open on the block outside the station.

In 1880 the city council of Brussels decided to let the fairs at Grand Place, Place des Martyrs and Marché-aux-Grains merge into one single fair that would take place at Boulevard du Midi. The most important fair in Brussels, it has evolved from offering such 19th Century fair favorites as wrestling matches, fortune telling and organ grinders to roller coasters, bumper cars and cotton candy.

Turn away from the train station and walk one block along Boulevard Poincare to the square on the left.

Point 7: Square de l'Aviation and Social Security Administration Building

The memorial here commemorates entertainers who gave their lives for Belgium during wartime.

Walk into the square towards the Art Deco building. It is the former home of Belgium's Social Security administration. Commissioned in 1911 and expanded in 1930, it has recently been renovated and currently houses war victims' services and the center for the study of war and contemporary society.

Follow rue Lambert Crickx to the right of the building, cutting across Square Pequeur at the end of rue Lambert Crickx. Turn right at the vacant lot, at one time a tram depot. You are now on rue Gheude.

Look down the right-hand side of the street for the sign of the man tipping over in his chair. It is No. 56, Cantillon Brewery and the Brussels Gueuze Museum.

Point 8: Cantillon Brewery

You are in Anderlecht, one of the 19 municipalities that forms Brussels. Occupied by humans settling along the Senne River in the Stone and Bronze Ages, the area became a theological center in the Middle Ages, home to Erasmus among others. In the 18th and 19th Centuries, workshops and small factories dotted the Anderlecht landscape as it took on an industrial character. During this time, its population boomed as residents from other parts of Brussels were forced to relocate because of urban development. Anderlecht was close to where their jobs were.

Among Anderlecht's industries was brewing.

Before the introduction of the steam engine and industrial refrigeration in the 19th Century, beer production resulted from natural fermentation, a process in which brewers are dependent upon wild airborne yeasts. Lambic beer is the only beer in the world still produced by natural fermentation. Cantillon Brewery is one of the few lambic brewers to still employ natural fermentation using the same techniques from centuries ago rather than more modern industrial technology.

Walk though Cantillon to see each step that comprises the lambic process. The cooling stage is Belgium's unique contribution to brewing. The mixture of wort is pumped into a large copper vessel where during Brussels' cold nights from late October to early April the natural fermenting agents (bacteria and yeast) interact with the wort beginning the inoculation process. The brew master at Cantillon opens and closes the shutters managing the flow of outside air to control the cooling process. Experts say the Senne River valley is the only place in the world offering the unique combination of temperature, humidity and air born micro-organisms to produce lambics on a consistent basis. The micro-organisms from the Senne River Valley are found nowhere else.

After the wort has sufficiently cooled, the brewers pump it into wooden barrels where the wild yeasts react with sugars in the wort resulting in spontaneous fermentation. The process releases carbon dioxide in such a violent manner, that the barrels are not sealed for three or four weeks to prevent them from exploding. Slow fermentation will continue in the barrel for as long as three years. By contrast, industrial brewing processes use stainless steel vessels and refrigeration systems to control fermentation in pils.

After enjoying your sample(s) of Cantillon which comes with the tour, exit the brewery turning left on rue Gheude retracing your steps to Boulevard M. Lemonnier.

No need for a debrief since three of the stops served beer.

Return: Once reaching Boulevard M. Lemonnier, either continue to walk along the boulevard or take the Metro at Lemonnier to the Bourse or De Brouckere.

Walk 13
Schaerbeek

The Donkey Village

**Length of Walk: 2 hours
without museums or debrief
Museum Options: Autrique House •
Schaerbeek Museum of Beer**

Connecting Dots: In the 2nd Century, roads built by Roman troops crisscrossed the area north of the marsh land around the River Senne, today's Schaerbeek. The written history of Schaerbeek dates to 1120 when the bishop of Cambrai recognized the Scarenbecca church north of Brussels. In the early 14th Century, as part of the Duchy of Brabant, a Church to Saint Servais was built and the area made a hunting ground and game preserve. In 1540, there were 112 houses and 600 Schaerbeek inhabitants whose main occupation was the growing of vines and vegetables. Starting in the 1570s and continuing for two centuries, army after army passed through Schaerbeek. They competed for the roadways with the donkey carts bringing Morello cherries to the city's breweries for the making of krieg. In 1879, a new Saint Servais Church was built near the old one. In 1905 Avenue Louis Bertrand was laid out to herald a new, tree-filled residential district for the city's burgeoning middle classes, many of whom employed the period's best architects to design their new homes. Gustave Strauven, François Hemelsoet and Henri Jacobs were three of the architects who reinvented family houses, apartment buildings and educational buildings here in the Art Nouveau style.

Starting point: Entrance to Metro at Parc. Exit the Metro and leave the park, crossing rue de la Loi directly in front of you.

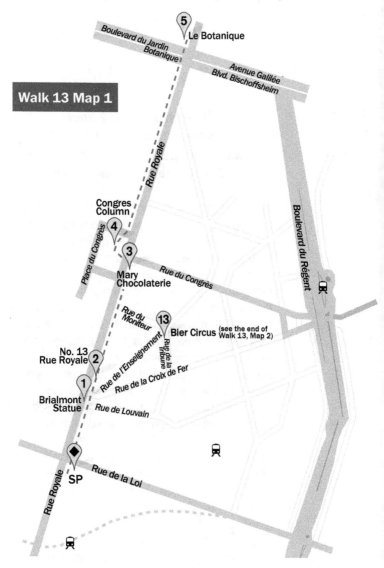

Point 1: Brialmont Statue

Walk along rue Royale to the first intersection where a statue of Henri-Alexis Brialmont stands. Brialmont was a 19th Century Belgian army officer, politician and writer best known as a military architect and fortress designer. Brialmont was especially associated with the Congo Free State. Leopold II retained him to design fortresses for the king's personal African possession.

Point 2: No. 13 Rue Royale

Further along rue Royale is an Art Nouveau gem. The flower shop at No. 13 built in 1898 was designed by Paul Hankar, one of the principal architects who practiced in the Art Nouveau style in Brussels at the end of the 19th Century. His training as a sculptor and early work as a furniture maker can be seen in the use of wood and curves, especially at the entrance. His design here is a temple to the curve.

Hankar and other Art Nouveau designers united flowing natural forms with angular contours. It was an alternative to the eclectic architectural style dominate in the earlier 19th Century that created new works by mixing historical forms. Art Nouveau architects rejected 19th Century design as being too ornamental, insisting that function dictate form.

Art Nouveau raised craft-based decorative arts to the same level of importance as the classical arts of painting and sculpture. A forerunner of modern design, Art Nouveau architecture considered buildings "total works of the arts." In its pure form, such as the flower shop, each element of the exterior and interior design celebrates good craftsmanship and draws from the same architectural vocabulary.

No. 17 is also an interesting shop, not for Art Nouveau although it does have curves. E. J. Binet et Fils dates from 1876. The company is a long-time Belgian arms merchant which today focuses on products for the high end safari market. Similarly, a few more stores up from Parc is a façade with an extended wooden window.

Keep walking along rue Royale away from Parc.

Point 3: Mary Chocolaterie

In 1919 chocolate maker and self-described chocolate lover Mary Delluc opened a business at No. 73 on rue Royale, a location carefully selected because of its proximity to the Royal Palace. The shop was on the route the king took when commuting to and from his residence in Laeken. Also, it was in the middle of walks taken by nobles and the bourgeois living along rue Royale who hoped to meet royal personages. To draw the attention of potential customers, Mary's shop windows featured decorations adapted to the seasons. On the inside, fitting with its Art Deco design, walls were decorated with hammered glass, rolled glass made nontransparent by embossing it on one side to resemble beaten metal.

Never married, Mary gave full attention to her business. By creating a chocolate shop that doubled as a tea room, Mary was able to share her enthusiasm with wealthy women and more importantly could discover the chocolates her customers most liked, listing each visitor's favorites in a guestbook.

A stickler for quality, she was known to send back a consignment of cocoa beans if they failed to meet her standards. What made her pralines famous was the ingredients of the fillings: The finest caramel, creams, gianduja, black chocolate, milk, coffee, almond paste, walnut paste pistachio paste, fruit paste, liqueur, candied fruit, dragees. She also invented chocolate langues de chat (cat tongues), small flat pieces of pure chocolate slightly rounded at the ends and slightly curved.

A marketing innovator, Mary's hand-crafted chocolate boxes often covered with plain silk or painted became collector's items. Representing femininity, a drape is repeated in all Mary shops and is featured in every gift box through the carefully folded and delicately placed tissue paper.

In 1942 Mary was awarded the title of "Certified Royal Warrant Holder of Belgium," an honor renewed in 1990 and 1994.

Point 4: Congres Column

Across rue Royale stands a tall column topped by a statue of King Leopold I. Inaugurated in 1859, the Congres Column conceals a spiral staircase of 193 stairs. Engraved on the column are important dates and names associated with the first Belgian National Congress and passages from the Belgian Constitution, Europe's most liberal when it was adopted in 1831. The four statues at the base represent the four fundamental liberties described in the Constitution: Union, Worship, Press and Education. The lions guarding the monument are another reference to the Constitution that declares the lion to be the state's coat of arms.

In 1922, Belgium buried five of its unknown soldiers from World War I to commemorate the war dead. An eternal flame lies atop their tomb. A second memorial plaque was added after World War II to honor that war's Belgian victims. In 1998 a third plaque was added to recognize Belgian soldiers killed in the service of peace since 1945.

Point 5: Le Botanique

Continue north for a few more blocks. You will pass by a garden adjacent to a big building, Le Botanique.

At the turn of 19th Century Europe, it was common for businessmen to finance private companies for the pursuit of public interests with the aim of increasing the prestige of their respective cities. With the city of Brussels short of funds to operate its botanical garden near where the National Library is today, a syndicate purchased land in a rural area where cherries were grown for kriek. They relocated the exhibits and constructed an orangerie in the Neoclassical style with pavilions and gardens surrounding it. Their vision was to create a national institution of science.

The timing was not good. A year after its 1829 opening, the building was severely damaged when Dutch troops used it as an encampment during the Belgian Revolution of 1830. With a new government in place following Belgian independence, the company reopened the complex. But perceived as a Dutch institution from its being founded when The Netherlands ruled the lowlands, the company was denied government support. The new regime considered the gardens little more than a playground for nobility, not useful to the country's agriculture. Short of cash, the company sold off part of the land allowing construction of Gare du Nord. It also engaged in various commercial activities, selling its plants and hosting fairs, concerts and dances. By the 1860s with the aging buildings requiring renovation, the Belgian government took over the company.

Fortuitously, the purchase coincided with the Belgian government's desire to create a National Botanic Garden. Several months before it bought the company, the government purchased some 300,000 preserved plant specimens from a private collector in Munich to create a national center for the classification of organisms. Now Belgium had a botanic collection and a building to house it.

During the construction of the north-south rail juncture in 1939, the gardens were mutilated. After the Second World War and recovery years, the National Botanic Garden moved in 1958 to the suburbs. In 1984 the building here reopened as the Botanical Garden of Brussels, a cultural center for the hosting of events. Thirty of the 52 statues that decorated the gardens in the 19th Century remain.

Continue along rue Royale for a few more blocks, walking towards the church.

Point 6: De Ultieme Hallucinatie

De Ultieme Hallucinatie is the green building on the left at rue Royale 316. Originally built in 1850 in the Neoclassical style, the building was redecorated in the early 20th Century under the eye of architect Paul Hamesse to a contemporary geometrical Art Nouveau style.

The front room is in the Art Nouveau empire style with Greek motifs. The middle room is in the French Art Nouveau style. In back, the brasserie occupies the former garden with a marble floor that replaced moss and ferns. The bar is where the orangery or greenhouse was. Train benches designed by Henry Vandevelde for the Belgian railways in the 1930s provide the seating. Beer of choice here is Achel, the smallest of the Trappist breweries. Try the Extra Brune or Blond.

Walk north to the church standing in the divide of rue Royale.

Point 7: Rue Royale

Take a moment to stand outside the front of the church looking down rue Royale. Schaerbeek is where two Roman roads converged linking north central Europe to Cologne and the rest of the Roman Empire. Before the mid-19th Century the street was known by residents as Donkey Avenue for the continuous flow of donkey-pulled carts carrying sour Morello cherries into the city for breweries to make krieg beer. Until the end of 18th Century, Schaerbeek was entirely rural. The street was renamed rue Royale when the road was expanded on the western side of the church to provide passage between the Royal Palace and the Royal Grounds at Laeken.

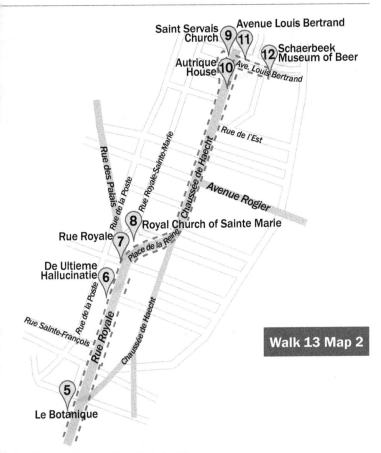

Point 8: Royal Church of Sainte Marie

Église Royale Sainte-Marie, founded as a Roman Catholic parish church, resides in what is now a Turkish dominated section of Brussels. Built from 1845 to 1885 on what were early Roman fortifications, the church was designed by Louis van Overstraeten and built in an eclectic style combining influences from Byzantine and Roman architecture. The dome is decorated with stars, and the bronze doors feature 32 engraved panels. The Four Evangelists and their symbols can also be found within the building's design. The windows were designed and created by the Belgian stained glass artist, Jean-Baptiste Capronnier.

Brussels is second only to Dubai as the most cosmopolitan city on the planet. As of 2016, Brussels had 1,187,890 residents, 411,025 of which were foreign nationals. Two-thirds of those are from a country in the European Union, with Moroccans and Turks following.

In the decades following World War II, Belgium lacked manpower to fuel its industries. To add workers, Belgium signed agreements with Morocco and Turkey. Many of the new workers eventually settled in Brussels with their families for construction and transport jobs. This policy foreign workers ended with the economic crisis of 1974.

Face the church and walk to the right side of the church. Take the 92 Tram north. Exit at the second stop, Saint Servais.

Point 9: Saint Servais Church

The original Saint Servais church was built in the 14th Century down the hill from the present-day church. It was the historical center of the village of Schaerbeek. The church's patron saint was Servatius of Tongeren, an Armenian who served as bishop of Tongeren in the 4th Century. Tongeren, located in the southeastern corner of the Flemish region of Belgium, is the oldest town in Belgium and the only Roman administrative capital to have been created within the borders of today's Belgium.

The church's construction began in 1871, based on plans drawn by architect Gustave Hansotte in the Gothic style. Its inauguration took place in 1876. Among the remarkable works in the church are the baptismal font, Neoclassical organ and the altar, the communion rail, pulpit and stalls carved by Guillaume Goyers.

Point 10: Autrique House

Walk back along Chaussee de Haecht, retracing the route the tram took. At No. 266 is an Art Nouveau masterpiece open to the public Wednesday to Sunday from noon to a last admission at 5:30 PM.

In 1893 Horta was 32 years old. He had completed an internship with Alphonse Balat and designed several houses in Ghent. Now in Brussels, he embarked on his professional career. Soon after Horta's arrival, Eugene Autrique, a friend and engineer at Solvay, asked him to design a house. Autrique's demands were simple: "not a single luxury, not a single extravagance, an inhabitable basement-floor, a dignified vestibule and staircase hall, the living and dining room nicely connecting, a first floor with bath and toilet (which wasn't common in those days) and a second floor for children and servants." The Autrique house became the first manor house designed by Victor Horta.

The elements that marked Horta's distinctive style are already apparent: Integration with the street, wall-decorations of varying thickness, co-existing symmetrical and asymmetrical shapes, and revolutionary use of metal. At around the same time, Horta designed the Tassel Hotel, one of his most famous works. The style that would soon be known as Art Nouveau began to take hold.

Walk back along Chaussee de Haecht to Saint Servais Church.

Point 11: Avenue Louis Bertrand

Schaerbeek boasts many Art Nouveau gems. Avenue Louis Bertrand running down the hill from the church is home to many of them. The avenue is named after a Belgian writer and politician who died in Schaerbeek in 1943.

Walk down the street stopping at the big vase in the middle.

Construction of the Avenue Louis Bertrand in the early 20th Century destroyed the village center and the ancient Saint Servais church. The church had not been used since the new Saint Servias church opened in1876.

When the avenue was laid out in 1905, the city of Schaerbeek commissioned a contest to encourage architects to design homes of great diversity. The result is the eclectic collection of residences seen today. Sgraffito, ceramics and stained glass turrets grace the avenue. Sgraffito is a technique used for wall décor that is produced by applying layers of plaster tinted in contrasting colors to a moistened surface and creating a drawing by scratching the plaster.

The vase of Bacchanalia stands in the place of the ancient church. A work of Godfried Devreese commissioned by Raoul Warocqué, one of Brussels foremost industrialists, the vase is a symbol of Belgium's break from its traditional past to a new era of commerce and scientific invention. Warocqué was a staunch defender of liberal and sectarian views in the predominately conservative Catholic country of Belgium. It was not by accident he decided to place the urn where the ancient church had been.

Walk down Avenue Louis Bertrand to the next intersection. Number 65's colorful tiles evoke the look of the neighborhood that disappeared. Among the other notable Art Nouveau houses on the street are: No. 1-2, No. 43, No. 53-61, No. 98-104 Residence Brusilia.

Point 12: Schaerbeek Museum of Beer

At Avenue Louis Bertrand 33-35 across from the vase is the Schaerbeek Museum of Beer. Located in what was a school for machinists, the museum features more than 2,000 Belgian beer glasses and 2,000 Belgian beer bottles along with associated marketing materials. It also has a small bar and tables if you feel the urge for a beer and a rest.

Return to the top of the hill to take the 92 Tram to debrief. Head in the direction of the center city, exiting at Congres, 5 stops away, where the Congres Column stands. (Be forewarned the Debriefing Point that follows is closed on weekends. Stay on the tram to return to Parc and the Metro if it is Saturday or Sunday.)

Point 13: Bier Circus

Cross rue Royale making a left at the first street, rue du Congres. Go one block. Turn right onto rue de L'Enseigment. After walking past the Cirque Royal, an entertainment venue, Bier Circus awaits you at the corner. It is marked on Map 1 in Walk 13.

If it is not a weekend when Bier Circus is closed, this is the perfect place to debrief and enjoy a specialty cooked with Belgian beer. Try a Vanderghinste Oud Bruin, a brown ale from Flanders if for no reason to see the faces of the two happy men in straw hats on the label.

Return: Turn left after exiting Bier Circus along rue de L'Enseigment. You will soon find yourself on rue Royale where you can take the Metro at Parc.

Walk 14
Tervuren

Aboard the Tram

**Length of Walk/Ride: 2.5 hours
without museums or debriefs**

**Museum Options: Tram Museum •
Royal Museum of Central Africa**

**Tour Option: Vintage Tram Ride
from the Tram Museum**

Connecting Dots: In Medieval times, small villages began to appear outside the fortification walls of Brussels. As the city grew and the walls fell into disrepair, residential neighborhoods took shape. In the north was Schaerbeek, whose farms supplied the cherries for krieg beer. To the south and southeast, emerged Ixelles and Saint-Gilles where successful industrialists, merchants and professionals engaged young architects to design town mansions. To the west of the city was Anderlecht, the Medieval home to Erasmus that grew to be an industrial center with laborer housing. To the east, the Leopold Quarter and Etterbeek became upscale destinations with town mansions, squares and an English garden and zoo. With the opening of Avenue Tervuren for the 1897 international exhibition and the construction of Avenue Louise in 1864, trams made even further locations in the east attractive destinations for wealthy Brusselites to live and to play.

Starting Point: Underground Metro station at Montgomery. Follow the signs within the Metro station to find Tram 44.

Point 1: Tram to Tervuren

This is a half-hour ride, not a visit. The 44 Tram emerges from the underground station at Montgomery to follow Avenue de Tervuren.

Commissioned by King Leopold II, construction of the avenue was completed in 1897 to coincide with the Brussels International Exhibition held in Cinquantenaire Park. Some of Brussels' most luxurious town homes began to appear along the avenue.

The 1897 exhibition, an official World's Fair, was no small affair. It featured more than 10,000 exhibits from 30 nations, of which 22 were represented officially. There were approximately 3,000 exhibits from France, the largest foreign participant. Like for the 1888 fair, a competition was organized by the Belgian government in which prize money was offered for answers to some 400 questions posed to seek solutions to problems depicted through the exhibits. They ranged from the social, such as an educational program to prevent alcohol abuse among students, to the technical, like a system of frost-proof water hydrants for use on roadways.

Popular features of the exhibition included the Brussels kermesse, a reconstruction of the old city replete with a 14th Century wall, a Renaissance-style gate designed by Belgian architect Paul Saintenoy, and reproductions of three famous city fountains – the Manneken-Pis, the Spitter (le Cracheur), and the Three Virgins (les Trois Pucelles). The exhibit for the Congo Free State, a personal posses-sion of King Leopold II, featured a model native village. An alpine exhibit employed special technical effects to allow visitors to experi-ence an actual mountain excursion.

The fair closed on November 8, 1897, after attracting some six million visitors.

Point 2: Palais Stoclet

Past the tram's second stop after emerging from underground, look to the right in the direction of travel for a large box-shaped complex with a tower. This is Palais Stoclet, the former residence of an early 20th Century banker. The female figures standing next to what looks like the dome of a mini skyscraper distinguishes it from its neighbors.

Designed by the Austrian architect Josef Hoffman, the home was built from 1905 to 1911 as a total work of art, inside and out. Hoffman designed every detail, from the exterior's white Norwegian marble with gold leaf trim to the interior's ebony side boards and chandeliers hung with pearls. Influences of Art Nouveau are encapsulated within a geometric form. The design is such that when inside you are continually drawn into the axes of the house, a perfectly logical use of the space. The Stoclet family fiercely protects the residence from the public. It is said the interior remains exactly as it was in 1911.

Point 3: Foret de Soignes

Enjoy the ride. After passing through residential areas, Tram 44 winds through the Foret de Soignes, the most significant remnant of an ancient European forest.

Foret de Soignes was part of the Silva Carbonaria, "charcoal forest," a dense collection of beech trees that formed a natural boundary between tribes populating present day France, Belgium, and Germany. It extended to the fortification walls of Brussels.

Charcoal fueled the smelting furnaces that were used to forge the iron found along river banks on the edge of the forest. The Belgae traded the iron weapons they manufactured for goods from their relatives the Celts who lived in southeast England.

Beginning in the Middle Ages through the 18th Century, the Dukes of Brabant used the forest outside the walls as their royal hunting grounds. This saved the area's natural beauty from large scale settlements.

Over time, timber cutting greatly reduced the size of the primeval forest, including in no small measure in 1805 when Napoleon Bonaparte ordered 22,000 oaks cut down to build the Boulogne flotilla for the invasion of England, an attack that was to be financed from sale of France's land in North America. Later, troops of William I of the Netherlands continued the deforestation for firewood.

The Forest of Soignes played a significant part in the Battle of Waterloo, about 15 kilometers (9 miles) from Brussels. From the time of the Romans, conventional battle strategy held to not position troops in front of woodland because it hampered the ability to retreat. Napoleon repeatedly criticized the Duke of Wellington's choice of battlefield because the forest was to Wellington's rear. We know how that turned out.

After the Belgian Revolution, the new Belgian government incorporated the forest as royal grounds for its new king. Today the forest consists mainly of European beeches and oaks with several trees more than 200 years old. The Bois de la Cambre, the city park beginning at the terminus of Avenue Louise, was formed out of the forest in 1842.

Today, you can see duck ponds, trails and bike paths as you travel through the forest.

Point 4: Tervuren

Towards the end of the ride, you enter Flanders, outside the Brussels district. The terminus is Tervuren, 10 kilometers (6 miles) to the east of Brussels. Long before becoming a wealthy suburb, Tervuren was a destination for pilgrims visiting the site of Saint Huburtus's death. Beginning in the Middle Ages, Tervuren hosted hunting lodges built by the Dukes of Brambant and which later became home to royal residences.

Exit here. The tram will reverse for the return trip. Before you return, there is time for a debrief and perhaps a museum visit.

Point 5: Royal Museum of Central Africa

A Debriefing Point and museum are located about 300 m past Tram 44's terminus. Walk along the main road to reach them. The museum, Royal Museum of Central Africa, reopened in 2018 after a major renovation.

In the 1890s, Belgium ranked fifth among nations in volume of foreign commerce. To draw attention to the nation's standing, Belgium hosted a World's Fair in 1897.

The main grounds for the exhibition were in the Parc du Cinquantenaire. An adjunct to the exhibition, the Pavilion of the Colonies, was built on the King's Royal grounds in Tervuren. It did not matter that Belgium only had one colony, the Congo Free State. Two new transport connections linking Parc du Cinquantenaire with Tervuren were part of the master plan: The elegant Avenue de Tervuren and the tram line.

The Berlin Conference of 1884-85 recognized the Congo Free State as a personal possession of the King of Belgium. By hosting the 1897 International Exhibition, the king sought to attract investors in his new colony. Also, the king wanted the Belgian populace to better know his far away country. He dreamed of more conquests.

The Tervuren exhibition displayed ethnographic objects, stuffed animals, and in the "Hall of the Great Cultures" Congo's most important export products: Coffee, cacao and tobacco. The building was designed by the Belgian architect Albert-Philippe Aldophe and the classical gardens by French landscape architect Elie Lainé. In the main hall, Georges Hobé designed a distinctive wooden Art Nouveau structure to evoke the forest using Bilinga wood, an African tree. Outside, a copy of an African village was built in which 60 Africans lived in zoo like conditions.

In 1898 the Palace of the Colonies became the Musée du Congo, and the exhibits became permanent. It was then scientific research at the museum took off. But due to the avid collecting of Belgian naturalists, the collection soon grew too large for the museum and enlargement was needed. Léopold II's solution was as usual grand. He built not only a larger museum but also Chinese and Japanese pavilions, a congress center, and a World School. They form today's complex.

Construction on the new museum started in 1904, following the Neoclassical palace architecture style of French architect Charles Girault who had also designed Petit Palais for the 1900 Paris World's Fair. Large gardens extended into the Tervuren Forest. King Albert I officially opened the museum in 1910 as The Museum of the Belgian Congo, a reference to the new name of the colony given in 1908 when ownership was transferred to the country from King Leopold II. In 1952 the adjective "Royal" was added. For Expo '58, a large building was constructed to receive African personnel.

In 1960 the museum again changed names to The Royal Museum for Central Africa. It had to because the Belgian Congo had ceased to exist when the Congo gained its independence. It was renamed Republic of Congo-Léopoldville. Reflecting on the harsh treatment of natives by Leopold and the hasty retreat by the Belgian government in 1960 after failed attempts to hold elections for an orderly transition of power, some call it a museum of arrogance and ignorance.

Point 6: Le Chalet Vert

Even if you don't wish to visit the museum, there is a good road house directly across the street from the museum's entrance. Le Chalet Vert (The Green Cottage) serves brasserie fare. Next store is a small hotel run by the same family since the 1890s.

It is a good time to enjoy a saison, the Belgian farmhouse ale. Saisons are common in the French-speaking area Wallonia and parts of Flanders. Brewed by Belgian farmers to serve as refreshment for their seasonal workers or saisonniers, the strongest of these beers seldom exceeded 5% ABV. Typically, they were consumed throughout the day.

Each farm made their own ale, giving it a distinctive flavor from the various grains cultivated at the farm and the use of homemade herbal mixtures known as gruits. While in most of Europe hops began replacing gruit a thousand years ago, partially due to their antiseptic properties, in Belgium many farmers continued using herbal mixtures along with hops. The use of herbs, and later spices, added the distinctive flavoring for which Belgian beers are known.

Like many other types of regional beers, farmhouse ales lost favor in the 19th Century as mechanical refrigeration changed the economics of brewing and lagers dominated sales in stores and bars. The two World Wars further disrupted local brewing. New production techniques allowing for a consistent product has enabled saison to make a commercial comeback with Saison DuPont being Belgium's most well-known brand.

Head back to the tram stop, where you will re-board Tram 44. Rather than returning to the city, exit at the Tram Museum.

Point 7: Tram Museum

The Tram Museum is in Woluwe, a wealthy municipality bordering on Foret de Soignes. The building was constructed in 1897, the same year Avenue de Tervuren opened. It housed the many trams that fed routes serving different parts of Brussels. After the opening of the Brussels Metro in 1969 and its expansion in the 70s, the depot became less important.

Vintage trams make special tours of the city departing from the museum, usually on Sundays. Visit the Tram Museum's website for information and reservations.

After leaving the museum, return to the tram stop. Go to the opposite side of the tram tracks from where you exited Tram 44. This time board the 94 Tram for the journey back into the city.

Point 8: Franklin Roosevelt Avenue

Tram 94 follows Boulevard du Souverian and later Franklin Roosevelt Avenue adjacent to the Foret de Soignes into Bois de la Cambre and Solbosch, home of the French-Speaking Free University of Belgium (ULB). The tram then turns onto Avenue Louise and enters the center city.

Franklin Roosevelt Avenue is dotted with terraced multi-story housing with the set-back window style common in the early to mid-20th Century Brussels. The upscale area's development followed construction of the avenue and the tram line. Interspersed are small homes with front and side yards. Like the terraces found on apartment buildings, they are reminders of the Bruxellois' love of garden space, a passion that fueled the rapid growth of the Brussels suburbs. Some homes along the route are diplomatic missions.

If you have sharp eyes, watch on right side in the direction of travel for No. 86, Maison Delune, named for the architect Leon Delune. Combining Art Nouveau, eclectic and Byzantine styles with a five-dome design, it is the only remaining building from the World's Fair of 1910. Soon after its opening it became the leading jazz venue in the city. The sgraffiti is by Paul Cauchie, the best known of the sgraffiti artists.

Point 9: World's Fair of 1910

No sooner than when the World's Fair of 1897 closed, Belgium began planning to host a fair to celebrate the 75th Anniversary of the country's founding. Eventually, it was decided an exhibition would be held in Liege in 1905 followed by a Brussels World's Fair in 1910.

Preparations for the Brussels fair began in earnest in 1907 when the Belgian government approved annexation to the city of land in the Foret de Soignes east of Bois de la Cambre, land that had been cleared of trees a century earlier by Napoleon's invading army.

Approval was contingent on streets being laid out and the land developed after the fair closed. The avenue you are on now, Avenue of the Nations as it was then called, was built to provide access from the city whether by automobile, horse or tram.

Twenty-one nations participated in the 1910 World's Fair. For the first time, exhibits were grouped along functional lines such as electricity, education, textiles, engineering and women's labor rather than by industry. In August, a fire engulfed the grounds, destroying the British exhibits, Parisian pavilion, race track, zoo and recreation of an old Brussels district like had been created for the 1897 fair. It seemed Belgians preferred to recreate their city rather than preserve it.

Point 10: Bois de la Cambre

After about a dozen stops from when you boarded, you will pass the Hippodrome, the city's horse racing track on the opposite side of the avenue. Dating from 1875, the now abandoned facility recalls the area's importance as a recreational destination when the laying of the tram routes provided access to outlying parks from the center city.

The Hippodrome sits at the southern end of the Bois de la Cambre, the city park named after an ancient abbey founded by a Benedictine nun. The abbey land was sold by the Belgian government to the city in 1842. The Bois de la Cambre was laid out in 1861, but convenient access to it had to wait until 1864 when the city annexed a strip of land that allowed for the construction of an avenue to reach it.

Franklin Roosevelt Avenue runs along the park's eastern edge. In all, Bois de la Cambre occupies 1.23 square kilometers of land (about one half square mile). In a section called The Englishman's Lawn, a bronze plaque was placed in 1965 by the British Ambassador to mark the spot where a 150 years earlier British soldiers played a cricket match on the eve of the Battle of Waterloo.

Soon you will pass by the Free University of Brussels on the same side of the avenue as the tram route.

Point 11: Free University of Brussels

The Free University of Brussels has been in various places around the city since its founding in 1834, including in buildings that in 1923 were demolished for construction of Central Station. In the 1920s the university began concentrating its facilities in Le Solbosch, the land to the east of today's Franklin Roosevelt Avenue. This included relocation of the city's scientific institutions from Leopold Park in 1921. Some 26,000 students are enrolled at university campuses (ULV for French speaking students and ULB for Flemish). In 1910 the school's football team won the bronze medal at the Olympics.

Point 12: Toll Booths

Past the university campus and at the northern end of the Bois de la Cambre, the tram makes a sharp turn. Take a quick look away from the turn. Two Neoclassical buildings flank each side of the road entering the park. They were originally toll booths, constructed in 1835 for use at the Porte de Namur. They were moved here soon after the Brussels entry tax was abolished in 1860.

The tram is now heading down Avenue Louise into the center city.

Point 13: Ixelles

You are in Ixelles, one of nineteen municipalities that comprise the Brussels Region of Belgium. The word is a derivation of Else, meaning alder woods. Alder is the tree family to which birch belong.

In 1795, the ruling French regime proclaimed Ixelles an independent commune. By 1813, it only had 677 residents. But in the years following the removal of the fortifications surrounding Brussels and the emergence of trams and street cars, the population soared. Ixelles became so fiercely independent that it delayed the extension of Avenue Louise from the City of Brussels to the Bois de la Cambre for more than 20 years in the mid-19th Century. When the avenue was completed, the community had been split in two: One side to the north of Louise and the other, smaller section to the south.

By 1900, Ixelles' population had swelled to 58,000, including artists, celebrities and prosperous businessmen who hired architects to design distinctive townhomes. Living in a first ring suburb was all the rage at the turn of the last century. Compared to the newer suburbs you have traveled through riding the tram there is less visible green space, but hidden gardens and parks in the rear of townhomes are common.

Point 14: Avenue Louise

The tram is gliding into the center city along Avenue Louise.

Development quickly followed the city of Brussels' annexation of the avenue's required land in 1864. A double line of chestnut trees was planted. Elegant town homes appeared. In the early 20th Century a tram line was installed on one side of the avenue with the other side remaining for horse traffic. The center was later converted for automobile use. The elegant appeal of the street began to wane when apartment buildings appeared in the 1930s. The trend accelerated when underpasses for automobile traffic were constructed for the 1958 World's Fair.

If you continue along Avenue Louise, you will be surrounded by Brussels' finest shops, but on this trip, you will leave the tram before entering the shopping district.

Exit at the Bailli stop.

Point 15: Pam Pam at Place du Chatelain

Bailli is the 2nd stop after you have turned onto Avenue Louise. Walk back to rue de Chatelain and turn right. A few blocks down tucked in amid restaurants and bars is Pam Pam on rue de l'Aqaueduc. It used to be named Le Duc. Perhaps it will be renamed when you read this. Regardless, beer surely will be served, and it is a Debriefing Point because of the atmosphere of Place du Chatelain. Wednesday nights are especially popular with oyster stands set up in the square. The café serves Tongerlo, either blond or dark at 6.0 ABV.

Return: Walk back to Avenue Louise and take the 93 or 94 Tram back to the Metro at Louise.

CPSIA information can be obtained
at www.ICGtesting.com
Printed in the USA
BVHW060401020822
643544BV00023B/2503